CQRS

The Example

Mark Nijhof

CQRS
The Example

Mark Nijhof

This book is for sale at http://fohj.in

This version was published on 2013-04-12

ISBN 978-1484102879

This is a Leanpub book. Leanpub empowers authors and publishers with the Lean Publishing process. Lean Publishing is the act of publishing an in-progress ebook using lightweight tools and many iterations to get reader feedback, pivot until you have the right book and build traction once you do.

©2013 Mark Nijhof

Contents

Miscellaneous — 1
    The cover 1
    Lean Startup for Developers 2
    To Work Remote 4

CQRS à la Greg Young — 5
    Queries (reporting) 8
    Commands (executing behavior on the domain) 9
    Command Handler 11
    Internal Events (capturing intent) 11
    Domain Behavior 12
    Domain Event 13
    Internal Domain Event Handler 13
    The Domain Repository 14
    Domain Repository Contract 15
    Data Mining 15
    External Events (publishing, letting others know) 15
    Eventual Consistency 16
    Specifications 17
    Some other benefits 20
    Finally 20

Domain Events — 21
    Using domain events for state change 22
    Getting the state changes 25
    Loading historical domain events 26
    The base class 27
    Aggregate entities 27
    Finally 30

CONTENTS

Domain State   31

Event Sourcing   33

Event Versioning   35

Scalability   43

Specifications   45
    Black box 45
    The BaseTestFixture 46
    The BaseTestFixture<TSubjectUnderTest> 47
    The PresenterTestFixture<TPresenter> 51
    CQRS and Event Sourcing 57
    Where is Should? 62
    Finally 62

Using conventions with Passive View   63
    Passive View 63
    The View 63
    The Presenter 66
    The Magic 68
    Reflection 72
    The Specifications 73

The Ubiquitous Language is not Ubiquitous   77

Convention over Configuration   79
    Configure your Conventions 79
    Not just for framework code 79

Trying to make it re-usable   81

    Convention over Configuration 83

    Why have everything protected? 84

    Reflect only once 85

    Conventional limits 85

    Current state 85

    Finally 86

Miscellaneous

The cover

They say; You judge a book by its cover, and therefore I am really happy to say that the CQRS book got a new cover.

The cover was generously provided by Sebastian from Leanpubcovers[1]. He also created the covers for my other writing project Lean Startup for Developers[2]. I highly recommend talking to him if you are also writing your own Leanpub book.

---

[1] http://leanpubcovers.com
[2] http://ls4d.com

Lean Startup for Developers

I have been building software professionally since 2000. One thing that is strikingly clear to me is; the amount of waste that is being created in our industry. We build and build without knowing that what we build is actually valuable. Will they use it? Will they pay for it? We just don't know!

So, there is the Lean Startup to the rescue. We now know that we should build a Minimal Valuable Product or MVP, instead of going all the way. But, now I hear things like; "Our MVP will be ready in a few months". Is it really necessary to wait several months before you can validate your ideas? I don't think it is!

We have come so accustomed to long running projects that we think delivering something in a month is fast. So, this book is about creating a different mindset, and about using the right tools. It is about accepting that building a MVP is not the same as building a product. This book is based on my own experiences, starting Inqob and Random Manager. Two startups still in their early phases.

Who is it for?

The bundle is mostly written for developers, it contains both the non-technical and the technical book. If you can relate to any of these points then the book might be right for you:

- You are thinking of building your own product, but you don't know where to start?
- You have already started your own adventure, and you would like to hear someone else's experiences running their own startup.
- You have no plans on starting something on your own, but you like the Lean Startup ideas and would like to apply them in your day to day work.
- You are non-technical, but would like to learn about what goes on inside the head of a technical person.

Go to: http://ls4d.com[3]

---

[3] http://ls4d.com

To Work Remote

Have you ever wondered what it would be like to work full-time remote?

I have just accepted a new job, which is 100% remote. I will be documenting my findings while I start walking the path of freedom, the happy parts but also the sad parts. This is not the story of an experienced remote worker. It won't be about best practices and how to's, I have no knowledge about this yet. If you are looking for that, then I suggest waiting for 37signals remote book.

But if you want to look through a little window, into the life of someone who is about to start working remotely on a full-time basis. Maybe just to see if this could be something for you as well? Then wait no more and start experiencing it for yourself, I will be your proxy.

Go to: http://toworkremote.com[4]

---

[4] http://toworkremote.com

CQRS à la Greg Young

I have had the pleasure of spending a 2 day course and many geek beers with Greg Young talking about Domain-Driven Design specifically focussed on the Command and Query Responsibility Segregation (CQRS) pattern. Greg has taken Domain-Driven Design from how Eric Evans describes it in his book and has adapted mostly the technical implementation of it. Command Query Separation (CQS) was originally thought of by Bertrand Meyer and is applied at object level

> Bertrand defines CQS as: every method should either be a command that performs an action, or a query that returns data to the caller, but not both. In other words, asking a question should not change the answer.

Greg however takes this same principle but he applies it to the whole architecture of a system, clearly separating the write side (Commands) from the read side (Queries) of the system. The write side is what we already know as the domain, containing all the behavior which is what makes the system valuable. The read side is specialized towards the specific reporting needs, think for example about the application screens that enables the users to execute domain behavior, but also any traditional reporting needs are provided by the read database.

So lets take a quick look at the overall architecture before we dive into the details:

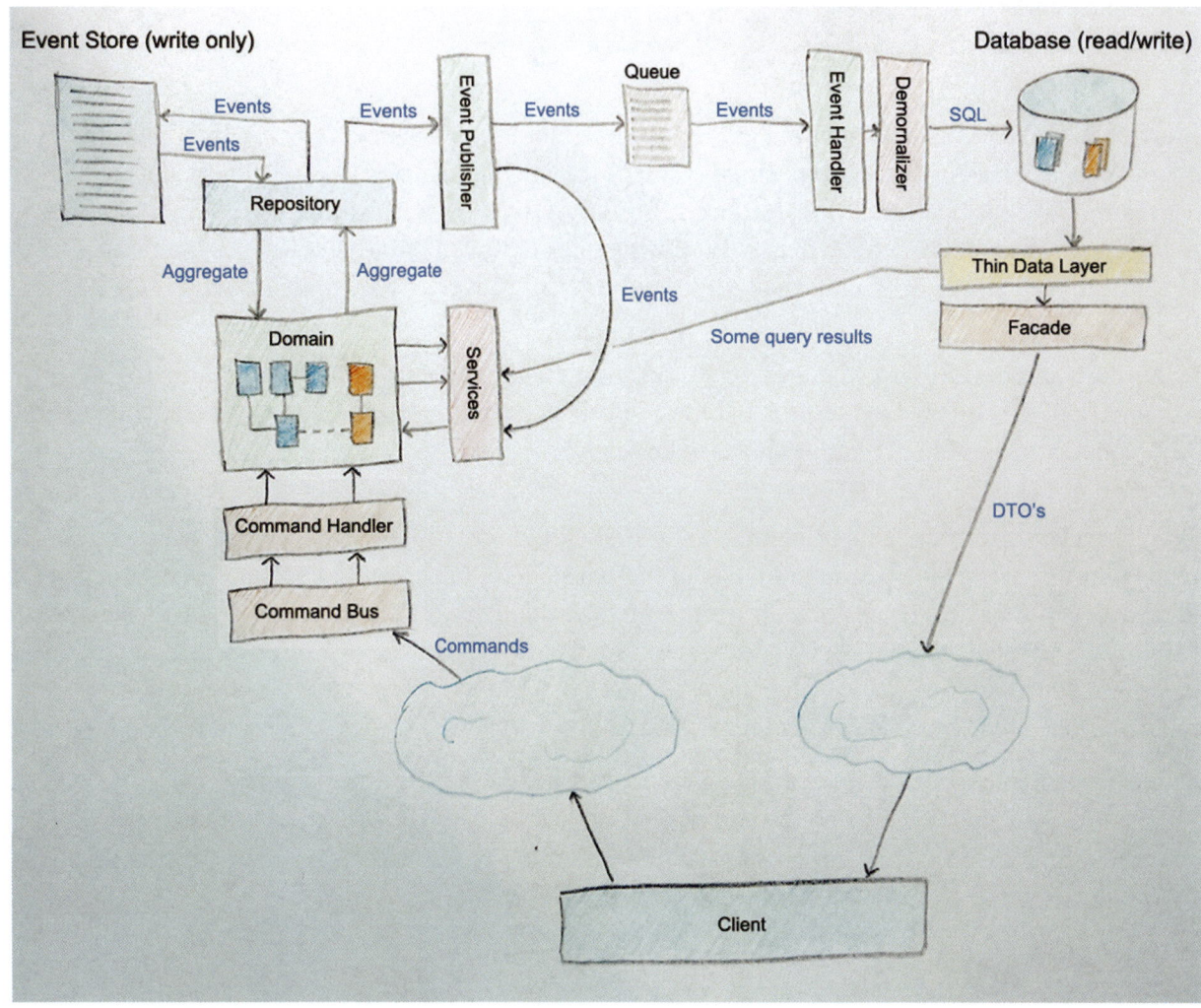

You have to excuse me for not using Visio to make this drawing, but I really didn't feel like tackling yet an other layer of complexity tonight. At least I did the labels in typed text, so it is readable. I will discuss this architecture in 4 phases, the order I choose is what I believe is the natural way your would think about this. In the end you will see that the whole principle is rather simple. Really.

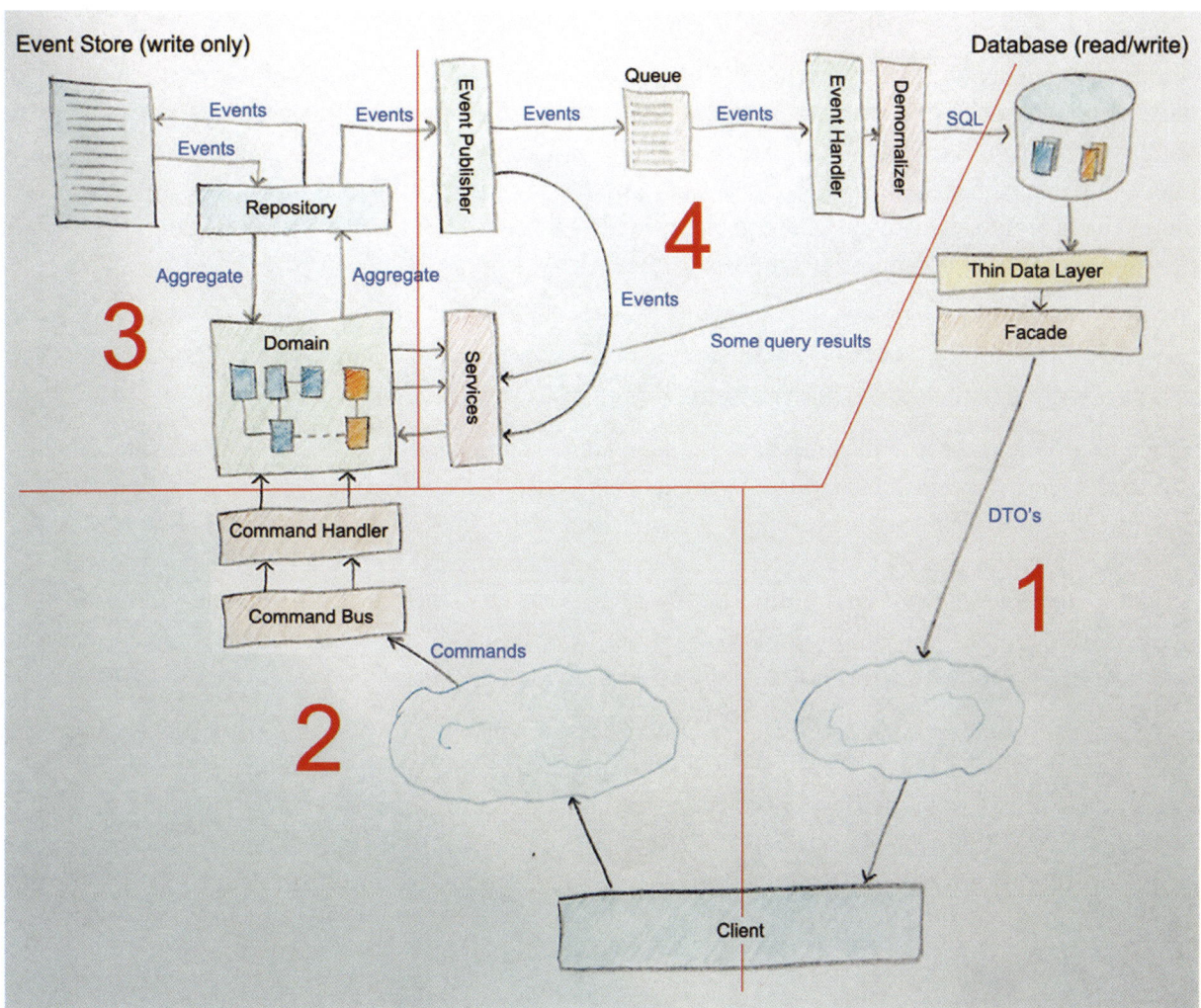

1. Queries
2. Commands
3. Internal Events
4. External Events (Publishing)

In order to understand this type of architecture better I decided to build an example application; I will use this example in this chapter to demonstrate the different aspects of the architecture to you.

The example has already been released in the wild (ok I meant the DDD group on Yahoo) and can be found here: http://github.com/MarkNijhof/Fohjin[5]

Queries (reporting)

The first part I would like to discuss is the reporting needs of a system, Greg defines any need for data from the system as a reporting need; this includes the various application screens which the user uses to base his decisions on. This seemed like a strange statement at first, but the more I think about it the more sense it makes. This data is purely used to inform the user (or other systems) about the current state of the system in the specific context of the user so that they can make certain decisions and execute domain behavior.

These reports will never be updated directly by the consumer of these reports, the data represents the state of the domain, so the domain is responsible for updating it. So all we really do on this side is report the current state of the system to who or what ever needs it.

When an application is requesting data for an specific screen than this should be done in one single call to the Query layer and in return it will get one single DTO containing all the needed data. Now because of this specific use of the data it makes sense to order and group it in such a way that is determined by the needs of the system. So we de-normalizing the data trying to make a single table reflect a single screen or usage in the client application. The reason for this is that data is normally queried many times more than domain behavior is being executed, so by optimizing this you will enhance the perceived performance of the system.

Here you may choose to use an ORM like NHibernate to facilitate the reading from the database, but considering that you would only be using a very small percentage of the capabilities of a proper ORM you may not need to go that way at all. Maybe going for Linq2Sql of even as Greg suggested using reflection to assemble the SQL statements directly from the DTO's (using reflection and Convention over Configuration makes this rather simple) is perhaps a better solution for the problem. This will be up to you and probably depends on specific scenario and what you feel comfortable with.

In the example that I created to demonstrate this type of architecture I choose for using reflection of the DTO's because I wanted to put the emphasis on the CQRS implementation and not on the ORM implementation.

The more traditional reporting needs will also get its own database schema and the data there will be optimized for that need as well, so in the end we will end up with quite a bit of duplication of the data, but that is all right. The process that is responsible for updating the data in the different databases will make sure that this happens in the correct way, we will go over this in a later part of this post.

---

[5]http://github.com/MarkNijhof/Fohjin

Commands (executing behavior on the domain)

Lets first consider what would normally happen after receiving a DTO; the user would make changes to the data and save this back on the DTO. This DTO then gets shipped back to the back-end, converted into an entity and the ORM will make sure that the changes are persisted into the database.

This would result in loosing some very valuable information; the Why did this change happen? You completely loose the intent the user had when he changed the data, and this is one of the things Greg's implementation of CQRS is solving.

CQRS as the name indicates uses Commands, these commands are created on the client application and then send to the Domain layer. Lets take an example: A customer from a bank comes in the office and tells the person behind the desk that he needs to change his address. And instead of just getting the customer information and making the changes directly in the address fields, the bank employee firsts asks the question; Why would you want to change your address? The most likely response would be because the customer has moved, but it could also be because there is an error in his address and that all his mail ends up with his downstairs neighbor. Now these are two completely different reasons to update a customer address. Why could this be important? Well granted the example is rather silly, but lets assume the bank wants to know how many customers go to a competitor after moving? How loyal are our customers, should we keep sending them specific information after they have moved x miles away? Right this information is completely lost in our original way of working, but when using commands and events (more on events later) we maintain the original intent of the action. So after asking the question the customer answers that he has indeed moved and the bank employee selects the "Customer has moved" in the application and gets the ability to change only the address. When clicking save a CustomerMovedCommand will be created with only the changed address and is send to the domain.

We also get one other great benefit from using these commands and that is that these commands are easy to communicate with our client while building or working on the system. Because our clients would most likely use these types of behavior when explaining what they want to accomplish. Al do Greg thinks times have changed, "Our grand failure", but it should really be the case that our clients talk their own domain language. When using these commands we can start talking the same language even in the code.

That is what Domain-Driven Design is all about, instead of doing something technical like update client, it is actually describing the process that the user uses into the code like; the client has moved.

```csharp
namespace Fohjin.DDD.Commands
{
    [Serializable]
    public class ClientIsMovingCommand : Command
    {
        public string Street { get; private set; }
        public string StreetNumber { get; private set; }
        public string PostalCode { get; private set; }
        public string City { get; private set; }

        public ClientIsMovingCommand(
          Guid id,
          string street,
          string streetNumber,
          string postalCode,
          string city) : base(id)
        {
            Street = street;
            StreetNumber = streetNumber;
            PostalCode = postalCode;
            City = city;
        }
    }
}
```

All these commands will be send to the Command Bus which will delegate each command to the command handler or command handlers. This also effectively means that there is only one entry point into the domain and that is via the Bus. The responsibility of these command handlers is to execute the appropriate behavior on the domain. Close to all of these command handlers will have the repository injected to provide the ability to load needed the Aggregate Root on which then the appropriate behavior will be executed. Usually only one Aggregate Root will be needed in a single command handler. Later we will also take a closer look at the repository as it is different from your ordinary DDD repository.

Command Handler

```
namespace Fohjin.DDD.CommandHandlers
{
    public class ClientIsMovingCommandHandler
      : ICommandHandler<ClientIsMovingCommand>
    {
        private readonly IDomainRepository _repository;

        public ClientIsMovingCommandHandler(
           IDomainRepository repository)
        {
            _repository = repository;
        }

        public void Execute(ClientIsMovingCommand compensatingCommand)
        {
            var client = _repository.GetById<Client>(
               compensatingCommand.Id);

            client.ClientMoved(new Address(
               compensatingCommand.Street,
               compensatingCommand.StreetNumber,
               compensatingCommand.PostalCode,
               compensatingCommand.City));
        }
    }
}
```

As you can see a command handler has only one responsibility and that is to handle the one particular command by executing the appropriate domain behavior. The command handler should not be doing any domain logic itself. If there is a need for this than that logic should be moved into a service of its own. An example of this is in my example code is an incoming money transfer, more about that later.

Internal Events (capturing intent)

So finally we have arrived at the actual domain, the client has requested a certain view of our domain, has received the appropriate report DTO and has made a decision which resulted into a command being published. The appropriate command handler has then loaded the correct Aggregate Root and executed the appropriate domain behavior. So now what?

Now we are going to separate the domain behavior from the state changes resulting from this domain behavior including the triggering of external behavior. This would not be much different from how you would do this now, first verify the normal guards, do what you have to do, but don't set any internal state, and don't trigger any external behavior (Ok the last part is more an optional thing to consider, state is the key here). Instead of writing these state changes directly to the internal variables you create an event and fire it internally. This event as well as the method name of the behavior should be descriptive in the Ubiquitous Language of the domain. Then the event will be handled inside the domain Aggregate Root which will set the internal state to the correct values. Remember that the event handler should not be doing any logic other then setting the state, the logic should be in the domain method.

Domain Behavior

```
public void ClientMoved(Address newAddress)
{
    IsClientCreated();

    Apply(new ClientMovedEvent(
        newAddress.Street,
        newAddress.StreetNumber,
        newAddress.PostalCode,
        newAddress.City));
}

private void IsClientCreated()
{
    if (Id == new Guid())
        throw new NonExistingClientException(
            "The Client is not created no operations can be executed on it");
}
```

Domain Event

```csharp
namespace Fohjin.DDD.Events.Client
{
    [Serializable]
    public class ClientMovedEvent : DomainEvent
    {
        public string Street { get; private set; }
        public string StreetNumber { get; private set; }
        public string PostalCode { get; private set; }
        public string City { get; private set; }

        public ClientMovedEvent(
          string street,
          string streetNumber,
          string postalCode,
          string city)
        {
            Street = street;
            StreetNumber = streetNumber;
            PostalCode = postalCode;
            City = city;
        }
    }
}
```

Internal Domain Event Handler

```csharp
private void onNewClientMoved(ClientMovedEvent clientMovedEvent)
{
    _address = new Address(
      clientMovedEvent.Street,
      clientMovedEvent.StreetNumber,
      clientMovedEvent.PostalCode,
      clientMovedEvent.City);
}
```

The reason why we want these events is because they now become part of our persistence strategy, meaning that the only information we will be persisting of an Aggregate Root are the generated events. So if every state change is triggered by an event, and an internal event handler has no other logic then setting the correct state (and that means not even deriving other information from the data in the event), then what we can do then is load all historical events and have the Aggregate Root replay them all internally bringing back the original state of the Aggregate Root in exactly the same way it got there in the first place. It really is the same as replaying a tape.

One thing to note is that these events are write only, you will never add, alter or remove an event. So if you suddenly end up with a bug in your system which is generating wrong events, then the only way for you to correct this is to generate a new compensating event correcting the results of the bug. Of course you want to fix the bug as well. This way you have also tracked when the bug was fixed and when the effects of the bug where corrected.

By having this architecture we now basically solved the problem of loosing original intent, because we keep all events that have ever happened and these evens are intent revealing. An other very interesting thing is that now you have an audit log for free, because nothing will ever change state without an event and the events are stored and used in building up the Aggregate Roots they are guaranteed in sync with each other.

The Domain Repository

I mentioned before that the Domain Repository would be completely different from one that is normally the result of practicing DDD. Normally you would end up with very specific repositories allowing the request of all kinds of different information from the domain. But when using Greg's implementation of CQRS your domain is completely write only, so the repository only has to be able to Get an Aggregate Root by its Id and it must be able to save the generated events. You also completely get rid of any impedance mismatch between the domain and the persistence layer.

Domain Repository Contract

```
namespace Fohjin.DDD.EventStore
{
    public interface IDomainRepository
    {
        TAggregate GetById<TAggregate>(Guid id)
            where TAggregate : class, IOrginator, IEventProvider, new();

        void Add<TAggregate>(TAggregate aggregateRoot)
            where TAggregate : class, IOrginator, IEventProvider, new();
    }
}
```

The reporting repositories on the other hand would probably look much more like the traditional repositories from DDD.

So what happens when you have 100.000 events that need to be replayed every-time you load the Aggregate Root, that will slow down your system immensely. So to counter this effect you would use the Memento pattern to take a snapshot from the internal state of the Aggregate root every x number of events. Then the repository will first request the snapshot, load that in the Aggregate Root and then request all the events that have occurred after the snapshot, bringing it back to the original state. This is only an optimization technique you would not delete events that happened before the snapshot, that would pretty much defeat the purpose of this architecture.

Data Mining

One other really interesting fact about storing all the events is that you can replay these events at a later date and retrieve important business information from them. And you get this information from the start of the system, instead having to build-in some extra logging and wait a few months for reliable data.

External Events (publishing, letting others know)

Finally we are getting to the fourth part of this explanation (and I am saying this more for my own sake, pfff). So what happens here, looking back at what we have so far, we can read domain state and we can execute behavior and update the internal state of the domain. The obvious thing that is missing is a way to bring the reporting database in sync with the current state of the domain. The way we will be doing this is by publishing the internal domain events outside the domain. Then there are event handlers that pick up on those events and bring the reporting database in sync. This is a place where you could use an ORM, but in fact it is very easy to just generate the needed SQL statements and execute them.

Greg actually mentioned a really nice way of caching these SQL statements, he would batch them in a single batch and execute the batch if it gets older then x seconds, or (and this is the interesting part) whenever a read request came in. So when a read request comes in this SQL statement is appended to the batch and the whole thing is executed, ensuring that the read request will always have the latest data available to that part of the system. More on this below here.

The domain repository is responsible for publishing the events, this would normally be inside a single transaction together with storing the events in the event store.

Events are also used to communicate between different Aggregate Roots, I my example I am using a transaction from one account to an other account. Here I generate an event that money is being transferred to an other account, this event will reduce the balance of the current account. Later an event handler will make the same change in the reporting database. An other event handler will actually forward the transaction to a service which checks if the target account is a local account, else forwards a money transfer to a different bank (in my example the different bank is actually the same, but via a different route). But lets assume that the money transfer goes to an internal account, in that case the service will publish a money transfer received command in the command bus and the whole process continues in a different Aggregate Root. So in this case the command is not triggered from a GUI but from a different part in the system.

There is an other interesting fact in the scenario when money is received from an other bank, because a money transfer only has the account number to identify the target account and not the Aggregate Root Id (you can't expect foreign systems to know this, yes I know you can make this a natural Id as well) the money received service first needs to do a query to the reporting database requesting an account DTO where the account number is the same as the target account. When this is successful it will use the Id from the account DTO and put that in the command to be published.

But it doesn't stop there, as I mentioned before you could also have events that don't have any state change information but for example indicate that a message (Email, SMS or what ever, depends on the event handler) needs to be send to an user. And because you are using Domain Events for all this, everything will be stored in the Event Store, so you keep your history.

Eventual Consistency

Normally when beginning to implement CQRS you would start with a direct publishing mechanism so that storing the events and updating the reporting database happen in the same thread. When using this approach you have no problems with eventual consistency.

But when you system starts to grow you might get some performance problems and then you could start by implementing a bus disconnecting the publishing of the events and handling of these events. This means that it is possible and likely that your event store and reporting database are not completely in sync with each other, they are eventual consistent. Which means that it is possible that the user sees old data on his screens.

Depending on how critical this really is you can have different counter measures for this, which I will be going into in a different chapter as this is also not something the example provides.

Specifications

The specifications that you can write using this architecture is something that I really like, what you would do is talk to your client and ask him things about how he wants his process to work. So a possible scenario could be:

Withdrawing money from an account

So how would that go? Well the clients needs to have opened an account with our bank and he needs to have some money transfered on it in order to be able to withdraw money from it. And when this happens the balance of the account must be lowered to the correct amount. Ok so, given an account was opened, and a cash was deposited, when making a cash withdraw then we get a cash withdrawn event.

```csharp
namespace Test.Fohjin.DDD.Scenarios.Withdrawing_cash
{
    public class When_withdrawing_cash : CommandTestFixture<
      WithdrawlCashCommand,
      WithdrawlCashCommandHandler,
      ActiveAccount>
    {
        protected override IEnumerable<IDomainEvent> Given()
        {
            yield return PrepareDomainEvent.Set(
              new AccountOpenedEvent(
                Guid.NewGuid(),
                Guid.NewGuid(),
                "AccountName",
                "1234567890")).ToVersion(1);
            yield return PrepareDomainEvent.Set(
              new CashDepositedEvent(20, 20)).ToVersion(1);
        }

        protected override WithdrawlCashCommand When()
        {
            return new WithdrawlCashCommand(Guid.NewGuid(), 5);
        }

        [Then]
        public void Then_a_cash_withdrawn_event_will_be_published()
        {
            PublishedEvents.Last().WillBeOfType<CashWithdrawnEvent>();
        }

        [Then]
        public void Then_the_event_will_contain_the_amount_and_balance()
        {
            PublishedEvents.Last<CashWithdrawnEvent>().Balance.WillBe(15);
            PublishedEvents.Last<CashWithdrawnEvent>().Amount.WillBe(5);
        }
    }
}
```

Ok ok, but now we have the same story, only now there is not enough money on the account, then we should give an exception.

```csharp
namespace Test.Fohjin.DDD.Scenarios.Withdrawing_cash
{
    public class When_withdrawling_cash_with_to_little_balance
        : CommandTestFixture<
            WithdrawlCashCommand,
            WithdrawlCashCommandHandler,
            ActiveAccount>
    {
        protected override IEnumerable<IDomainEvent> Given()
        {
            yield return PrepareDomainEvent.Set(
              new AccountOpenedEvent(
                Guid.NewGuid(),
                Guid.NewGuid(),
                "AccountName",
                "1234567890")).ToVersion(1);
        }

        protected override WithdrawlCashCommand When()
        {
            return new WithdrawlCashCommand(Guid.NewGuid(), 1);
        }

        [Then]
        public void Then_acc_balance_to_low_exception_will_be_thrown()
        {
            CaughtException.WillBeOfType<AccountBalanceToLowException>();
        }

        [Then]
        public void Then_the_exception_message_will_be()
        {
            CaughtException.WithMessage(
              string.Format(
                "The amount {0:C} is larger than your balance {1:C}",
                1, 0));
        }
    }
}
```

The cool part here is that the whole domain is seen as a black box, you are bringing it to a certain state exactly the same way as it is used, then you publish a command just like your application would, and after that you verify that the domain publishes the correct events and that their values are correct. This means that you are never testing your domain in a state that it cannot naturally get to, which makes the tests more reliable.

Now imagine a parser that takes all the class names, underneath each class name it would print the events that occurred to get into the current state. Then you print the command that we are testing, and finally you print the method names that test the actual outcome. This would be a very nice readable specification that the client at least can understand.

Some other benefits

One last benefit I would like to highlight from using this type of architecture is how easy it is to split the work load between different team, more specifically between team with different hourly rates. The domain logic is something that needs to be right, this is where you would put your more expensive developers on, the ones that understand the business, understand good coding practices, you know what I mean. But the read side is not as important, sure it needs to be correct as well, but this is not where the value lies, this can be done quickly and in a year or two again. This is something you let the cheaper developers create, it doesn't require much domain knowledge all that is really important is that they need to know how the GUI needs to work, what commands they can use and what events to expect.

I think this is of great value for the business, something that is easily overlooked.

Finally

As you can see this is all very simple and straightforward. It is a different mindset, but once you enter this mindset you will notice that your applications will be much more behavioral versus CRUD. And hopefully our clients can move back into thinking about their business logic instead of the thinking about the CRUD way we have forced upon them. Also I would like to thank Greg Young for providing me with so much information and putting up with all my weird questions, and thank Jonathan Oliver and Mike Nichols for some improvements on the technical side.

Domain Events

As you may have seen in my previous chapter now our domain aggregate root is responsible for publishing domain events indicating that some internal state has changed. In fact state changes within our aggregate root are *only* allowed through such domain events. Secondly the internal event handlers are *not* allowed to have any sort of business logic in them, they are *only* supposed to set or update the internal state of the aggregate root directly from the data the event carries. Using these rules you completely separate the business logic from the state changes. This separation enables us to replay historical domain events without any business logic being triggered bringing it back to the same state as the original aggregate root.

Why is this important? Well now we can use these same domain events for our persistence using an Event Store, this pattern by Martin Fowler is called "Event Sourcing[6]". Obviously you don't want to process a credit card or send an e-mail every time you load an aggregate root from the event store. Also from the time the original domain event was recorded and when the aggregate root is loaded from the event store the business logic that decided a state change was needed could have changed, this should not affect the actual historical state change. So this separation is to be taken seriously.

Domain events can also be used to signal something to the outside world (taken from the aggregate roots view point) that something has happened without having an actual state change. When persisting our domain events we would not differentiate between those two different domain events.

All domain events should be named with the ubiquitous language in mind, meaning that they should closely represent what the user intended to do in the same language as the user would use to explain it to you. By keeping all these domain events we gain a huge amount of knowledge about what happened and why it happened.

This means that our aggregate root gets the added responsibility of tracking these domain events, but I don't see this as being any different then for example the proxy that NHibernate generates for you, except perhaps that it is not a proxy and that you have more control over what happens. But it is true your aggregate root has these added responsibilities.

So let us take a look at how the aggregate root provides this functionality, for obvious reasons we use a base class for this, but really all that is needed is that the aggregate root implements the following two interfaces:

---

[6]http://martinfowler.com/eaaDev/EventSourcing.html

```csharp
namespace Fohjin.DDD.EventStore.Storage.Memento
{
    public interface IOrginator
    {
        IMemento CreateMemento();
        void SetMemento(IMemento memento);
    }
}
```

The IOrginator interface is for the snapshot functionality which is an optimization technique for speeding up loading aggregate roots from the Event Store. As you can see it is using the "Memento" patter from the Gang Of Four[7] book. I wanted to get this interface out of the way first; it is not needed, but does provide a good optimization for loading aggregate roots.

```csharp
namespace Fohjin.DDD.EventStore
{
    public interface IEventProvider
    {
        void Clear();
        void LoadFromHistory(IEnumerable<IDomainEvent> domainEvents);
        void UpdateVersion(int version);
        Guid Id { get; }
        int Version { get; }
        IEnumerable<IDomainEvent> GetChanges();
    }
}
```

The IEventProvider interface is the most interesting interface of the two, this one defines how domain events can be retrieved from the aggregate root and how historical domain events can be loaded back. It also defines that each aggregate root must have an Id and a Version, both of these are used by the event store, the Id is obvious so I won't go into that, the version on the other hand may not be that obvious. The version is used to detect concurrency violations, meaning this is used to prevent conflicts that occur because between the time the command was send and the aggregate root was saved an other user or process has updated the same aggregate root. In this case we would throw an Concurrency Violation Exception which currently results in a rollback. In a future chapter I plan to look into how you could try to deal with these concurrency violations automatically.

Using domain events for state change

Now we will take a look at how these interfaces are implemented and how the implementation is used. The way I am going to go through the code is as if you where using R# going from method to

---

[7]http://c2.com/cgi/wiki?GangOfFour

method. So in order to get a more overall impression I would encourage you to look at the source code. The source code can be found here: http://github.com/MarkNijhof/Fohjin

Each aggregate root has to register the domain events and the internal event handlers with the base class. I am working on getting this as static information for the type since this will not change between different instances of the same type. As you can see I am registering the domain event type and an action to handle the specific type. As you can see the actions have the specific domain event as an input parameter.

```
private void registerEvents()
{
    RegisterEvent<ClientCreatedEvent>(onNewClientCreated);
    RegisterEvent<ClientMovedEvent>(onNewClientMoved);
}

private void onNewClientCreated(ClientCreatedEvent clientCreatedEvent)
{
    Id = clientCreatedEvent.ClientId;
    _clientName = new ClientName(clientCreatedEvent.ClientName);
    _address = new Address(
      clientCreatedEvent.Street,
      clientCreatedEvent.StreetNumber,
      clientCreatedEvent.PostalCode,
      clientCreatedEvent.City);
    _phoneNumber = new PhoneNumber(clientCreatedEvent.PhoneNumber);
}

private void onNewClientMoved(ClientMovedEvent clientMovedEvent)
{
    _address = new Address(
      clientMovedEvent.Street,
      clientMovedEvent.StreetNumber,
      clientMovedEvent.PostalCode,
      clientMovedEvent.City);
}
```

The RegisterEvent method is defined in the BaseAggregateRoot class, here is a little bit of interesting logic going on where basically a new action is defined that has an IDomainEvent as an input parameter, that is how they can all be stored in the same Dictionary. Then inside this action the provided action is invoked where the input value is cast from an IDomainEvent to the actual expected type TEvent.

```
1  private readonly Dictionary<Type, Action<IDomainEvent>> _registeredEvents;
2
3  protected void RegisterEvent<TEvent>(Action<TEvent> eventHandler)
4      where TEvent : class, IDomainEvent
5  {
6      _registeredEvents.Add(
7          typeof(TEvent),
8          theEvent => eventHandler(theEvent as TEvent));
9  }
```

So if we would write the example out of what is actually happening for the Client Created Event then it would look like this example below, and this is what is being stored in the _registeredEvents.

```
1  public void Delegate(IDomainEvent domainEvent)
2  {
3      onNewClientCreated(domainEvent as ClientCreatedEvent);
4  }
```

And below here is the private apply method that is being called from two different methods in the aggregate root base class. The method retrieves the action that is registered for the provided domain event, and than it invokes the action with the domain event as the input parameter. The apply method takes an IDomainEvent instead of the specific domain event and because of that we have the above mentioned logic.

```
1   private void apply(Type eventType, IDomainEvent domainEvent)
2   {
3       Action<IDomainEvent> handler;
4
5       if (!_registeredEvents.TryGetValue(eventType, out handler))
6           throw new UnregisteredDomainEventException(
7               string.Format(
8                   "The requested domain event '{0}' is not registered in '{1}'",
9                   eventType.FullName,
10                  GetType().FullName));
11
12      handler(domainEvent);
13  }
```

Let us take a look from where this apply method is being called, first we will look at some actual domain behavior in the aggregate root.

```
1  public void Withdrawl(Amount amount)
2  {
3      Guard();
4
5      IsBalanceHighEnough(amount);
6
7      var newBalance = _balance.Withdrawl(amount);
8
9      Apply(new CashWithdrawnEvent(newBalance, amount));
10 }
```

First we execute all our valuable domain logic, the business behavior. Then when we are satisfied that everything is ok and we know what type of state change we need to execute and we Apply a new domain event with the new internal state. The Apply method used here is a protected method on the BaseAgregateRoot. Btw there is nothing stating that there can only be one outcome, i.e. only one type of domain event being Applied.

```
1  protected void Apply<TEvent>(TEvent domainEvent)
2      where TEvent : class, IDomainEvent
3  {
4      domainEvent.AggregateId = Id;
5      domainEvent.Version = GetNewEventVersion();
6      apply(domainEvent.GetType(), domainEvent);
7      _appliedEvents.Add(domainEvent);
8  }
```

When we Apply a domain event we will first assign the aggregate root Id to the event so that we can keep track to which aggregate root this event belongs to. Secondly we get a new version and assign this to the event, this is to maintain the correct order of the events. Then we call the apply method which will make the state change to the aggregate root. And finally we will add this domain event to the internal list of applied events. This is very similar with the dirty check of NHibernate (the idea, not the actual implementation).

This is all what what is needed to execute domain behavior and keep track of the domain events that have been used to update internal state of an aggregate root.

Getting the state changes

So now we have build up some internal state changes and we want to persist them to some sort of medium. I am not going to discuss how to actually persist these state changes, that is for a later post, all I want to show you now is how to get them out of the aggregate root. How about we start with the method GetChanges :)

```
1  IEnumerable<IDomainEvent> IEventProvider.GetChanges()
2  {
3      return _appliedEvents
4          .Concat(GetEntityEvents())
5          .OrderBy(x => x.Version)
6          .ToList();
7  }
8
9  private IEnumerable<IDomainEvent> GetEntityEvents()
10 {
11     return _entityEventProviders
12         .SelectMany(entity => entity.GetChanges());
13 }
```

Here we simply return all the applied domain events, by tracking these domain events we in effect track all the state changes that have happened since the aggregate root was instantiated. Here we also request all the applied domain events from all entities. Than new order the domain events by version. After having received and processed all the applied domain events we should Clear the aggregate root from all applied domain events so they won't be persisted again.

```
1  void IEventProvider.Clear()
2  {
3      _entityEventProviders.ForEach(x => x.Clear());
4      _appliedEvents.Clear();
5  }
```

Just a quick word about the entity event providers, in some cases you want to have domain behavior inside entities that are part of the aggregate but are not the aggregate root. Well in this case you want to have those entities generate domain events as well, and you want to get those as well when getting all changes. Same when clearing the domain also the changes inside each entity event provider should be cleared.

Before saving the changes in the aggregate root is finalized we also need to update the version of the aggregate root. This version will match the version of the last applied domain event.

Loading historical domain events

In a next chapter I'll dig deeper into the event store but for now lets just assume you have a very nice way of storing these domain events and have the ability to retrieve them again.

As the IEventProvider interface nicely dictates there is a LoadFromHistory method that takes an IEnumerable<IDomainEvent> below here is the implementation of this method.

```csharp
void IEventProvider.LoadFromHistory(IEnumerable<IDomainEvent> domainEvents)
{
    if (domainEvents.Count() == 0)
        return;

    foreach (var domainEvent in domainEvents)
    {
        apply(domainEvent.GetType(), domainEvent);
    }

    Version = domainEvents.Last().Version;
    EventVersion = Version;
}
```

When you take a look in the for each loop you will notice that here we are calling apply again, please note that this is the private variant which is responsible for updating the internal state of the aggregate root and that these events are not added to the _appliedEvents collection, nor is the Id or Version updated. We don't want to save these events again. After applying all the historical domain events we update the aggregate root version to the version of the last event.

The base class

I am using a base class to provide this functionality to all the different aggregate roots using inheritance and I know there are different opinions about this. So I wanted to highlight that you can achieve the same results by using composition. Your aggregate roots still need to implement the interfaces, but the implementation can be provided by using composition.

An other thing is that all the public methods in the BaseAggregateRoot are explicate interface implementation. I do this because I want to hide these details for any piece of code that is using the aggregate root as is, only when dealing with persistence we use the interface and get access to the explicit interface methods. Nice and clean.

Aggregate entities

Ok I have already mentioned the term entities and entity event providers, and I would like to focus on them for a bit. An entity is an domain object that is part of the same aggregate as the aggregate root, but is not the aggregate root it self, is however it is managed by the aggregate root. We manage state changes in these entities in the exact same way as we do this in the aggregate root, so each entity is also an event provider. There is a different interface for the entities then for the aggregate root so they can not be confused among each other.

```
namespace Fohjin.DDD.EventStore
{
    public interface IEntityEventProvider
    {
        void Clear();
        void LoadFromHistory(IEnumerable<IDomainEvent> domainEvents);
        void HookUpVersionProvider(Func<int> versionProvider);
        IEnumerable<IDomainEvent> GetChanges();
        Guid Id { get; }
    }
}
```

You may have also noticed the hookup version provider method, remember it :)

The problem is that we should deal with the whole aggregate as a whole so all state changes need to be persisted within the same transaction. So we want to have a single point to access the internal state of the whole aggregate as well as a single point to load the history back into the whole aggregate. In order to achieve this the aggregate root needs to register all the entity event providers so it can track them. To enable that we have an additional interface for our aggregate root to implement.

```
namespace Fohjin.DDD.EventStore
{
    public interface IRegisterEntities
    {
        void RegisterEntityEventProvider(
            IEntityEventProvider entityEventProvider);
    }
}
```

Lets look at the implementation right away

```
void IRegisterEntities.RegisterEntityEventProvider(
    IEntityEventProvider entityEventProvider)
{
    entityEventProvider.HookUpVersionProvider(GetNewEventVersion);
    _entityEventProviders.Add(entityEventProvider);
}
```

Now this is only a very simple collection that hold references to IEntityEventProviders which is used in the previous shown GetEntityEvents method. So getting out the changes is relatively simple this way. I also created a special collection that will automatically register entities when they are added to the collection.

Remember I mentioned the HookUpVersionProvider method, well this is used to get a reference to the method from the aggregate root that deals with assigning a new version to each event. We want a reference to the same version generator that the aggregate root uses because then all the versions of each domain event will be in sequence independently is the aggregate root or an entity created it.

```
namespace Fohjin.DDD.Domain
{
    public class EntityList<TEntity>
        : List<TEntity> where TEntity : IEntityEventProvider
    {
        private readonly IRegisterEntities _aggregateRoot;

        public EntityList(IRegisterEntities aggregateRoot)
        {
            _aggregateRoot = aggregateRoot;
        }

        public new void Add(TEntity entity)
        {
            _aggregateRoot.RegisterEntityEventProvider(entity);
            base.Add(entity);
        }
    }
}
```

The collection takes a reference to the aggregate root it is part of in the constructor to be able to add each added entity event provider to the collection in the aggregate root.

Currently there is some duplication between the BaseAggregateRoot and the BaseEntity because they are inherited from different interfaces, I am sure there is some optimization possible there :)

There is finally one more thing to cover about this and that is how historical domain events are being passed into the correct entity, currently this is a bit ugly but I am working on a more elegant solution. Take a look at the code.

```csharp
private void registerEvents()
{
    // Registration of Aggregate Root event handlers

    RegisterEvent<BankCardWasReportedStolenEvent>(
      onAnyEventForABankCard);
    RegisterEvent<BankCardWasCanceledByClientEvent>(
      onAnyEventForABankCard);
}

private void onAnyEventForABankCard(IDomainEvent domainEvent)
{
    IEntityEventProvider bankCard;
    if (!_bankCards.TryGetValueById(
      domainEvent.AggregateId,
      out bankCard))
        throw new NonExistingBankCardException(
          "The requested bank card does not exist!");

    bankCard.LoadFromHistory(new[] { domainEvent });
}
```

So each entity domain event will be registered here as well and are all passed to one specific event handler (one specific event handler for each different entity type). What happens is that we check if the specific event provider is present in the collection by looking for the Id, when the requested event provider is found the historical domain event will be loaded using the load from history method on the event provider.

The problem here is that the information which events the entity can produce is already registered, and that is in the entities them self's. So by making that information statically available I should be able to auto register the entity event handlers.

Finally

I hope that this was a useful explanation of how the aggregate root works with the internal domain events, and that you would agree with me that it really is not very difficult. Next time I want to discuss the event store so we can take a look at persisting the domain events.

Domain State

This morning Aaron Jensen[8] asked a really interesting question[9] on Twitter "Should Aggregate Roots en Entities always keep their state if it is not needed for business decisions? Is firing events and relying on the reporting store enough?". He really made me think, Aaron thanks for that!

So for example you have some behavior on your domain that gets called when a customer moves, this behavior will publish a Customer Moved event containing the new address. If the domain does not use the address information for any decision making, does it then need to be persisted in the aggregate root?

I guess it would greatly depend on whether or not you are using Event Sourcing[10] to persist your published events (this is what I would suggest). If you do then I don't see a problem in skipping storing the address information in the aggregate root. Because if at a later time you need the address information to make some decisions then it is easy to retrieve this from the events when reloading the aggregate root from the event store. You just create the address property and an internal event handler to process the Customer Moved event. Just make sure you delete the snapshots first.

But if you do not store all the events that you publish, but instead store only a snapshot then I would not skip storing the new address information, because in the end the domain is responsible for the state, not the reporting side. In other words, you can rebuild the reporting side from the domain, but you cannot necessarily do the same in reverse. So if you don't store the address information and you need to rebuild the reporting store then you cannot do this.

So my conclusion is that the information should be available on the domain side. And when using CQRS and Event Sourcing to store the events instead of the internal state of the domain then that makes it possible to skip having the information in the domain structure, else not.

---

[8]http://codebetter.com/blogs/aaron.jensen/default.aspx
[9]http://twitter.com/aaronjensen/status/6454974718
[10]http://martinfowler.com/eaaDev/EventSourcing.html

Event Sourcing

So after reading this blog post by Rob Conery about Reporting In NoSQL[11] where he explains very well what the problem is when using a RDBMS for persisting the state of your domain, or really anything that is written with Object Orientation in mind.

His solution to the problem is to use a object database or a document database for persisting the state of your object structure. And I do agree that this is a valuable approach to solve the problem.

But I would like to talk about a different approach, which is called Event Sourcing[12]; a pattern thought of by Martin Fowler that, "Captures all changes to an application state as a sequence of events."

Hey that is interesting, so instead of trying to store the object tree in a whole, we just store all the individual state changes that the object tree encapsulates; meaning all the state changes that have happened during the complete lifetime of the object tree. These state changes are being represented in the form of events. And such an event is nothing more then a Plain Old CLR Object[13], so not an actual .Net event.

And the objects are also re-constructed from the same events by applying all the state changes that they represent, and thus coming back to the previous state in the identical way that it came there originally.

Now the interesting part with respect to persistence is that these events are being serialized using a technique you like (Binary, JSon or custom) and this serialized event (object) is persisted in an event store, and this event store will threat all serialized events equally.

This event store can be based on an object database, document database, file system or even a RDBMS, you basically need to have one collection that describes all the different objects that the event store has persisted this includes the Id and the Version. Then another collection will contain all the serialized events for each different object and they should be retrievable by the object Id ordered by their Version. So to simplify this, in a RDBMS this would mean 2 tables, in total.

So there is no impendence mismatch between the domain (object structure) and the persistence layer anymore. Which would mean that it is should pass Rob's criteria's as well.

But hey it doesn't stop there, you get a real audit log[14] for free a well. And you have the ability to replay all the events to abstract new information about certain state changes. For example a web store is in business for 6 months and now they would like to know when and where an item is being removed from the shopping cart. With an event store you will have this information from the start of the system, and you didn't have to think about it straight from the start.

And this also enables an easier swift to an Event Driven Architecture as well, because you can start publishing the events outside of the domain and have different behavior or processes react on them.

---

[11] http://blog.wekeroad.com/2010/02/05/reporting-in-nosql
[12] http://martinfowler.com/eaaDev/EventSourcing.html
[13] http://en.wikipedia.org/wiki/Plain_Old_CLR_Object
[14] http://martinfowler.com/eaaDev/AuditLog.html

In my example[15] I use a combination of CQRS and Event Sourcing and this makes a very powerful solution. I would recommend that when you are when applying CQRS you would do that in combination with Event Sourcing to get a very flexible system without much more complexity then just applying CQRS.

---

[15]http://github.com/MarkNijhof/Fohjin/tree/master/Fohjin.DDD.Example/

Event Versioning

When using Event Sourcing you store your events in an Event Store. This Event Store can only insert new events and read historical events, nothing more nothing less. So when you change your domain logic and also the events belonging to this behavior, then you cannot go back into the Event Store and do a one time convert of all the historical events belonging to the same behavior. The Event Store needs to stay intact, that is one of its powers.

So you make a new version of the original event, this new version carries more or less information then the original one. Lets take a look at a very simple example:

```csharp
namespace Fohjin.DDD.Events.Account
{
    [Serializable]
    public class CashWithdrawnEvent : DomainEvent
    {
        public decimal Balance { get; private set; }
        public decimal Amount { get; private set; }

        public CashWithdrawnEvent(decimal balance, decimal amount)
        {
            Balance = balance;
            Amount = amount;
        }
    }

    [Serializable]
    public class CashWithdrawnEvent_v2 : DomainEvent
    {
        public decimal Balance { get; private set; }
        public decimal Amount { get; private set; }
        public Guid AtmId { get; private set; }

        public CashWithdrawnEvent_v2(
            decimal balance,
            decimal amount,
            Guid atmId)
        {
            Balance = balance;
            Amount = amount;
            AtmId = atmId;
        }
```

```
32        }
33    }
```

This to me looks like a natural evolution for this type of event, so how do you deal with this. Because after having used the system, before adding this extension there have been many cash withdrawals. So all these events are in the Event Store, they cannot be altered, and when you retrieve an Aggregate Root from the Event Store all these historical events need to be processed in order to restore the internal state.

Now what you don't want is to maintain code in the Aggregate Root that knows how to handle these old event versions, sure one version is ok, but what about one hundred different versions? Also we are not just talking about just in the Aggregate Root, also the different event handlers need to be kept and maintained.

The better approach is to have a mechanism that you can hook-up with different event convertors. Then when an event is retrieved from the Event Store it first goes through this pipeline of convertors to be converted to the latest event version.

Now I wanted to do this properly and write some actual code for this, and then blog about it, but someone kept nagging me about it, so here is a very rough spike instead, first some tests:

```csharp
namespace Test.Fohjin.DDD.Spike
{
    public class Spike_test_1 : BaseTestFixture
    {
        private object ConvertedEvent;

        protected override void When()
        {
            ConvertedEvent = new EventConvertor()
                .Convert(new CashWithdrawnEvent(10.0M, 20.0M));
        }

        [Then]
        public void The_converted_event_is_the_latest_version()
        {
            ConvertedEvent.WillBeOfType<CashWithdrawnEvent_v4>();
        }

        [Then]
        public void The_converted_event_wil_contain_the_correct_data()
        {
            ConvertedEvent.As<CashWithdrawnEvent_v4>()
                .Balance.WillBe(10.0M);
            ConvertedEvent.As<CashWithdrawnEvent_v4>()
                .Amount.WillBe(20.0M);
            ConvertedEvent.As<CashWithdrawnEvent_v4>()
                .AtmId.WillBe(string.Empty);
        }
    }

    public class Spike_test_2 : BaseTestFixture
    {
        private object ConvertedEvent;

        protected override void When()
        {
            ConvertedEvent = new EventConvertor()
                .Convert(new CashWithdrawnEvent_v2(10.0M, 20.0M, "12345"));
        }

        [Then]
        public void The_converted_event_is_the_latest_version()
```

```csharp
            {
                ConvertedEvent.WillBeOfType<CashWithdrawnEvent_v4>();
            }

            [Then]
            public void The_converted_event_wil_contain_the_correct_data()
            {
                ConvertedEvent.As<CashWithdrawnEvent_v4>()
                    .Balance.WillBe(10.0M);
                ConvertedEvent.As<CashWithdrawnEvent_v4>()
                    .Amount.WillBe(20.0M);
                ConvertedEvent.As<CashWithdrawnEvent_v4>()
                    .AtmId.WillBe("12345");
            }
        }

        public class Spike_test_3 : BaseTestFixture
        {
            private object ConvertedEvent;

            protected override void When()
            {
                ConvertedEvent = new EventConvertor()
                    .Convert(new CashWithdrawnEvent_v3(10.0M, 20.0M, "12345"));
            }

            [Then]
            public void The_converted_event_is_the_latest_version()
            {
                ConvertedEvent.WillBeOfType<CashWithdrawnEvent_v4>();
            }

            [Then]
            public void The_converted_event_wil_contain_the_correct_data()
            {
                ConvertedEvent.As<CashWithdrawnEvent_v4>()
                    .Balance.WillBe(10.0M);
                ConvertedEvent.As<CashWithdrawnEvent_v4>()
                    .Amount.WillBe(20.0M);
                ConvertedEvent.As<CashWithdrawnEvent_v4>()
                    .AtmId.WillBe("12345");
            }
```

```csharp
85        }
86
87    public class Spike_test_4 : BaseTestFixture
88    {
89        private object ConvertedEvent;
90
91        protected override void When()
92        {
93            ConvertedEvent = new EventConvertor()
94                .Convert(new CashWithdrawnEvent_v4(10.0M, 20.0M, "12345"));
95        }
96
97        [Then]
98        public void The_converted_event_is_the_latest_version()
99        {
100            ConvertedEvent.WillBeOfType<CashWithdrawnEvent_v4>();
101        }
102
103        [Then]
104        public void The_converted_event_wil_contain_the_correct_data()
105        {
106            ConvertedEvent.As<CashWithdrawnEvent_v4>()
107                .Balance.WillBe(10.0M);
108            ConvertedEvent.As<CashWithdrawnEvent_v4>()
109                .Amount.WillBe(20.0M);
110            ConvertedEvent.As<CashWithdrawnEvent_v4>()
111                .AtmId.WillBe("12345");
112        }
113    }
114 }
```

So basically some tests to confirm the correct conversion from one event to another event, now below here is the full implementation:

```csharp
namespace Test.Fohjin.DDD.Spike
{
    public class EventConvertor
    {
        private Dictionary<Type, Func<object, object>> _convertors;

        public EventConvertor()
        {
            _convertors = new Dictionary<Type, Func<object, object>>();
            RegisterEventConvertors();
        }

        private void RegisterEventConvertors()
        {
            _convertors.Add(typeof(CashWithdrawnEvent),
                x => new CashWithdrawnEventConvertor()
                    .Convert((CashWithdrawnEvent)x));
            _convertors.Add(typeof(CashWithdrawnEvent_v2),
                x => new CashWithdrawnEvent_v2Convertor()
                    .Convert((CashWithdrawnEvent_v2)x));
            _convertors.Add(typeof(CashWithdrawnEvent_v3),
                x => new CashWithdrawnEvent_v3Convertor()
                    .Convert((CashWithdrawnEvent_v3)x));
        }

        public object Convert(object soureEvent)
        {
            Func<object, object> convertor;
            return _convertors.TryGetValue(
                soureEvent.GetType(),
                out convertor)
                    ? Convert(convertor(soureEvent))
                    : soureEvent;
        }
    }

    public interface IEventConvertor<TSourceEvent, TTargetEvent>
        where TSourceEvent : IDomainEvent
        where TTargetEvent : IDomainEvent
    {
        TTargetEvent Convert(TSourceEvent sourceEvent);
    }
```

```csharp
public class CashWithdrawnEventConvertor
    : IEventConvertor<CashWithdrawnEvent, CashWithdrawnEvent_v4>
{
    public CashWithdrawnEvent_v4 Convert(
      CashWithdrawnEvent sourceEvent)
    {
        var theEvent = new CashWithdrawnEvent_v4(
          sourceEvent.Balance, sourceEvent.Amount, string.Empty)
        {
            AggregateId = sourceEvent.AggregateId
        };
        (theEvent as IDomainEvent).Version =
          (sourceEvent as IDomainEvent).Version;
        return theEvent;
    }
}

public class CashWithdrawnEvent_v2Convertor
    : IEventConvertor<CashWithdrawnEvent_v2, CashWithdrawnEvent_v3>
{
    public CashWithdrawnEvent_v3 Convert(
      CashWithdrawnEvent_v2 sourceEvent)
    {
        var theEvent = new CashWithdrawnEvent_v3(
          sourceEvent.Balance, sourceEvent.Amount, sourceEvent.AtmId)
        {
            AggregateId = sourceEvent.AggregateId
        };
        (theEvent as IDomainEvent).Version =
          (sourceEvent as IDomainEvent).Version;
        return theEvent;
    }
}

public class CashWithdrawnEvent_v3Convertor
    : IEventConvertor<CashWithdrawnEvent_v3, CashWithdrawnEvent_v4>
{
    public CashWithdrawnEvent_v4 Convert(
      CashWithdrawnEvent_v3 sourceEvent)
    {
        var theEvent = new CashWithdrawnEvent_v4(
```

```
85                    sourceEvent.Balance, sourceEvent.Amount, sourceEvent.AtmId)
86                {
87                    AggregateId = sourceEvent.AggregateId
88                };
89            (theEvent as IDomainEvent).Version =
90                (sourceEvent as IDomainEvent).Version;
91            return theEvent;
92        }
93    }
94 }
```

This implementation is definitely not very elegant but hey it does show you how a possible solution would work. When building this yourself you might want to use conventions to auto register the convertors and chain them together during configuration so there is no need for the recursive functionality.

Also look at the jump from version 1 to version 4, this is an optimization to speed up the conversion. You would do this after a few versions, not for each version.

I'll be adding a proper solution to the example in the near future, something that you would just plug the convertors in and the system would figure out how to handle them itself.

Scalability

Scalability is one of the several different benefits you gain from applying CQRS and Event Sourcing to your application architecture. And that is what I wanted to take a closer look at in this post.

One of the first obvious ways to increase the performance of your system is to split the Command from the Query side by using a service bus or just a simple queue. So instead of one machine being responsible for both responsibilities you now have 2 machines.

Then you also get the ability to measure more precisely what the actual bottleneck is, normally your application queries for data many times more then that it is executing behavior. And there are already many well known approaches for scaling your reporting database so that is not what I would like to talk about, but I guess it is clear that this side can now be scaled-out individually from the command side.

Now the command side; because even if this is used many times less then the query side, the actual behavior may take much more time and or processing power.

There are two natural ways of splitting up the domain, the first one is by Aggregate Root type, so you can choose to place a single (or multiple) Aggregate Root type on a different server. The second way is by splitting-up a single Aggregate Root type by the Identity each individual instance has. Think of for example about splitting them up depending on the last number of the Id, even versus un-even.

So who decides? The decision needs to be made by the process that accepts the commands and passes them on to the command handlers, these command handlers can then be running on different machines and each machine may even have it's own Event Store.

This is a very flexible way of splitting-up your system into different components, and because of the Event Driven Architecture basically build-into this approach you will be able to trigger other behavior on different Aggregate Roots without added trouble.

Specifications

I received a couple questions about the Specification Framework that I use in the CQRS example[16] and thought lets talk about that for a bit. The first thing that should be underlined is that this is *not* a framework, they are a few classes and extension methods[17] that rely on NUnit[18] for the actual assertions and and Moq[19] for mocking of the dependencies. I got the initial bits from Greg Young at his DDD course which I extended a little bit for my specific needs.

I have the following base test fixture classes:

1. BaseTestFixture
2. BaseTestFixture<TSubjectUnderTest>
3. AggregateRootTestFixture<TAggregateRoot>
4. CommandTestFixture<TCommand, TCommandHandler, TAggregateRoot>
5. EventTestFixture<TEvent, TEventHandler>
6. PresenterTestFixture<TPresenter>

These different classes are all very specific towards a specific need, which is a direct opposite from what a framework usually provides.

Black box

I try my best to make my tests treat the subject under test (SUT) as a black box, meaning that in my tests I don't directly interact with the actual class that I am testing. Instead I want to trigger the behavior by executing behavior that lies further outside. The behavior that triggers the behavior on the SUT may be an actual implementation, or it could be a fake.

The same applies to the result of the behavior that gets tested, instead of verifying some state in the SUT I want to verify what happens outside of the SUT. So what matters is that I test the behavior not the state of the subject under test.

I also try to get further away from the SUT then its immediate usage. Doing so makes the tests less brittle for change. This in itself is not always an easy task, but I recommend you try it anyway.

---

[16]http://github.com/MarkNijhof/Fohjin/tree/f85a25181b4fa382bd3afbbbbcb08da891cc8e45/Fohjin.DDD.Example

[17]http://github.com/MarkNijhof/Fohjin/tree/f85a25181b4fa382bd3afbbbbcb08da891cc8e45/Fohjin.DDD.Example/Test.Fohjin.DDD

[18]http://www.nunit.org/index.php

[19]http://code.google.com/p/moq/

The BaseTestFixture

This is the simplest test fixture class that I have and I use this for and I actually don't use this anywhere in the example code, but it serves a really good basic overview of the semantics that are shared among the other test fixture classes.

```csharp
namespace Test.Fohjin.DDD
{
    [Specification]
    public abstract class BaseTestFixture
    {
        protected Exception CaughtException;
        protected virtual void Given() { }
        protected abstract void When();
        protected virtual void Finally() { }

        [Given]
        public void Setup()
        {
            CaughtException = new NoExceptionButOneWasExpectedException();
            Given();

            try
            {
                When();
            }
            catch (Exception exception)
            {
                CaughtException = exception;
            }
            finally
            {
                Finally();
            }
        }
    }

    public class GivenAttribute : SetUpAttribute { }

    public class ThenAttribute : TestAttribute { }

    public class SpecificationAttribute : TestFixtureAttribute { }
```

```
37     }
```

It is following the Given When Then (GWT) approach, and as you can see it is really simple. Also note that I introduced some other named attributes by simply inheriting from the default NUnit attributes, this was purely done to stay with the GWT approach.

Below here is an incredible KISS example of how you would use this BaseTestFixture, which I believe doesn't need further explanation. (I know I am misusing the term KISS here, but I thought if was fitting anyway).

The BaseTestFixture<TSubjectUnderTest>

Now we are getting into a more interesting case because now my subject under test is actually provided by the generic parameter of the base test fixture class. And to be honest this class is only used with 12 specifications out of the 122 specification classes. This is mostly because it is still a very generic solution, but again a nice way to ease into it.

```csharp
namespace Test.Fohjin.DDD
{
    [Specification]
    public abstract class BaseTestFixture<TSubjectUnderTest>
    {
        private Dictionary<Type, object> mocks;

        protected Dictionary<Type, object> DoNotMock;
        protected TSubjectUnderTest SubjectUnderTest;
        protected Exception CaughtException;
        protected virtual void SetupDependencies() { }
        protected virtual void Given() { }
        protected abstract void When();
        protected virtual void Finally() { }

        [Given]
        public void Setup()
        {
            mocks = new Dictionary<Type, object>();
            DoNotMock = new Dictionary<Type, object>();
            CaughtException = new NoExceptionButOneWasExpectedException();

            BuildMocks();
            SetupDependencies();
            SubjectUnderTest = BuildSubjectUnderTest();
```

```csharp
            Given();

            try
            {
                When();
            }
            catch (Exception exception)
            {
                CaughtException = exception;
            }
            finally
            {
                Finally();
            }
        }

        public Mock<TType> OnDependency<TType>() where TType : class
        {
            return (Mock<TType>)mocks[typeof(TType)];
        }

        private TSubjectUnderTest BuildSubjectUnderTest()
        {
            var constructorInfo = typeof(TSubjectUnderTest)
                .GetConstructors().First();

            var parameters = new List<object>();
            foreach (var mock in mocks)
            {
                object theObject;
                if (!DoNotMock.TryGetValue(mock.Key, out theObject))
                    theObject = ((Mock) mock.Value).Object;

                parameters.Add(theObject);
            }

            return (TSubjectUnderTest)constructorInfo
                .Invoke(parameters.ToArray());
        }

        private void BuildMocks()
```

```
68              {
69                  var constructorInfo = typeof(TSubjectUnderTest)
70                      .GetConstructors().First();
71
72                  foreach (var parameter in constructorInfo.GetParameters())
73                  {
74                      mocks.Add(
75                          parameter.ParameterType,
76                          CreateMock(parameter.ParameterType));
77                  }
78              }
79
80              private static object CreateMock(Type type)
81              {
82                  var constructorInfo = typeof(Mock<>)
83                      .MakeGenericType(type).GetConstructors().First();
84                  return constructorInfo.Invoke(new object[] { });
85              }
86          }
87      }
```

Wow there is *a lot* more going on here! You are right, because here I make the base test fixture responsible for instantiating the subject under test, including providing mocks for any dependencies that it may have. So it is an auto mocker as well, but the interesting part here is that it puts a reference of the injected mocks in a collection that you can access inside your tests by using the OnDependency<TType> method that returns a Moq object.

Take a look at a specification using this base test fixture class:

```
1   namespace Test.Fohjin.DDD.Scenarios.Receiving_money_transfer
2   {
3       public class When_receiving_a_money_transfer
4           : BaseTestFixture<MoneyReceiveService>
5       {
6           protected override void SetupDependencies()
7           {
8               OnDependency<IReportingRepository>()
9                   .Setup(x => x.GetByExample<AccountReport>(
10                      It.IsAny<object>()))
11                  .Returns(new List<AccountReport> {
12                      new AccountReport(
13                          Guid.NewGuid(),
14                          Guid.NewGuid(),
```

```csharp
15                         "AccountName",
16                         "target account number") });
17         }
18
19         protected override void When()
20         {
21             SubjectUnderTest.Receive(
22                 new MoneyTransfer(
23                     "source account number",
24                     "target account number",
25                     123.45M));
26         }
27
28         [Then]
29         public void Then_the_newly_created_account_will_be_saved()
30         {
31             OnDependency<IBus>().Verify(
32                 x => x.Publish(It.IsAny<ReceiveMoneyTransferCommand>()));
33         }
34     }
35 }
```

So the first thing you see is the method SetupDependencies that is requesting the mock object for injected type IReporintgRepository and it is using the Moq way of setting up the Mock object. This is only needed when in your specification you need the mocks to be setup in a specific way. I intentionally separated the SetupDependencies from the Given as they may be two different things. And in the actual test you see the usage of the OnDependency method again where its being used to verify that something was indeed triggered on the injected class.

Now indeed this is not really treating the subject under test as a black box, for example in the When I make a direct call to a method on the subject under test. So my test knows about this now, meaning when it changes I need to change this test as well. So lets take a look where I go a bit further into the black box mentality.

The PresenterTestFixture<TPresenter>

Here I am not going to show you the code of the PresenterTestFixture implementation as it is almost identical the the previous base test fixture. So lets go straight to an actual specification:

```csharp
namespace Test.Fohjin.DDD.Scenarios.Adding_a_new_client
{
    public class When_the_phone_number_of_the_new_client_is_saved
        : PresenterTestFixture<ClientDetailsPresenter>
    {
        private object CreateClientCommand;

        protected override void SetupDependencies()
        {
            OnDependency<IPopupPresenter>()
                .Setup(x => x.CatchPossibleException(It.IsAny<Action>()))
                .Callback<Action>(x => x());

            OnDependency<IBus>()
                .Setup(x => x.Publish(It.IsAny<object>()))
                .Callback<object>(x => CreateClientCommand = x);
        }

        protected override void Given()
        {
            Presenter.SetClient(null);
            Presenter.Display();
            On<IClientDetailsView>().ValueFor(
                x => x.ClientName).IsSetTo("New Client Name");
            On<IClientDetailsView>().FireEvent(
                x => x.OnFormElementGotChanged += null);
            On<IClientDetailsView>().FireEvent(
                x => x.OnSaveNewClientName += null);

            On<IClientDetailsView>().ValueFor(
                x => x.Street).IsSetTo("Street");
            On<IClientDetailsView>().ValueFor(
                x => x.StreetNumber).IsSetTo("123");
            On<IClientDetailsView>().ValueFor(
                x => x.PostalCode).IsSetTo("5000");
            On<IClientDetailsView>().ValueFor(
                x => x.City).IsSetTo("Bergen");
```

```csharp
            On<IClientDetailsView>().FireEvent(
                x => x.OnFormElementGotChanged += null);
            On<IClientDetailsView>().FireEvent(
                x => x.OnSaveNewAddress += null);

            On<IClientDetailsView>().ValueFor(
                x => x.PhoneNumber).IsSetTo("1234567890");
            On<IClientDetailsView>().FireEvent(
                x => x.OnFormElementGotChanged += null);
        }

        protected override void When()
        {
            On<IClientDetailsView>().FireEvent(
                x => x.OnSaveNewPhoneNumber += null);
        }

        [Then]
        public void Then_the_save_button_will_be_disabled()
        {
            On<IClientDetailsView>().VerifyThat.Method(
                x => x.DisableSaveButton()).WasCalled();
        }

        [Then]
        public void Then_create_client_command_will_be_published()
        {
            On<IBus>().VerifyThat.Method(
                x => x.Publish(It.IsAny<CreateClientCommand>())).WasCalled();

            CreateClientCommand.As<CreateClientCommand>()
                .ClientName.WillBe("New Client Name");
            CreateClientCommand.As<CreateClientCommand>()
                .Street.WillBe("Street");
            CreateClientCommand.As<CreateClientCommand>()
                .StreetNumber.WillBe("123");
            CreateClientCommand.As<CreateClientCommand>()
                .PostalCode.WillBe("5000");
            CreateClientCommand.As<CreateClientCommand>()
                .City.WillBe("Bergen");
            CreateClientCommand.As<CreateClientCommand>()
                .PhoneNumber.WillBe("1234567890");
```

```
80            }
81
82            [Then]
83            public void Then_overview_panel_will_be_shown()
84            {
85                On<IClientDetailsView>().VerifyThat.Method(
86                    x => x.Close()).WasCalled();
87            }
88        }
89  }
```

Again there is the setting up of a dependency in the beginning and then there is the Given method, Presenter in this case is the subject under test, so you can see that the specification still knows about the SUT in the Given, but you will notice that this is not used in either the When or the Then.

Hey what is that On thing in there? Well that is a very small DSL wrapping the Moq API. I did this to make it slightly more readable, and in this case it is very adapt towards working with a view and presenter. In the Given I am setting up my IClientDetailsView with the correct data, but I am also simulating that an event was triggered. This is not logic that the test is concerned about, all we do here is bring the view and the presenter in the correct state for this particular specification. So instead of setting these things directly on the presenter this will all be directed from the view.

Then in the When we again fire an event from the view, but in this case it is the going to trigger the behavior on the presenter that we want to verify. And in the Then methods we verify on the view again that the presenter actually did the correct things, but we also verify on other dependencies that the correct methods where called, in this case the IBus.

I am not completely happy with the mini DSL yet, but I think it is cleaner then the default Moq API. Just for those that are curious, here is the mini DSL which gets returned by the On method:

```csharp
namespace Test.Fohjin.DDD
{
    public class MockDsl<TType> where TType : class
    {
        private readonly IDictionary<Type, object> _mocks;

        public MockDsl(IDictionary<Type, object> mocks)
        {
            _mocks = mocks;
        }

        public ValueSetter<TType, TProperty> ValueFor<TProperty>(
          Expression<Func<TType, TProperty>> selector)
        {
            return new ValueSetter<TType, TProperty>(_mocks, selector);
        }

        public void FireEvent(Action<TType> fieldSelector)
        {
            if (!_mocks.ContainsKey(typeof(TType)))
                throw new Exception(
                    string.Format(
                        "The requested dependency '{0}' is not specified",
                        typeof(TType).FullName));

            var mock = (Mock<TType>)_mocks[typeof(TType)];
            mock.Raise(fieldSelector);
        }

        public Verifier<TType> VerifyThat {
          get {
            return new Verifier<TType>(_mocks); } }
    }

    public class Verifier<TType> where TType : class
    {
        private readonly IDictionary<Type, object> _mocks;

        public Verifier(IDictionary<Type, object> mocks)
        {
            _mocks = mocks;
        }
```

```csharp
        public void ValueIsSetFor(Action<TType> selector)
        {
            if (!_mocks.ContainsKey(typeof(TType)))
                throw new Exception(
                    string.Format(
                        "The requested dependency '{0}' is not specified",
                        typeof(TType).FullName));

            var mock = (Mock<TType>)_mocks[typeof(TType)];
            mock.VerifySet(selector);
        }

        public MethodVerifier<TType> Method(
          Expression<Action<TType>> selector)
        {
            return new MethodVerifier<TType>(_mocks, selector);
        }
    }

    public class MethodVerifier<TType> where TType : class
    {
        private readonly IDictionary<Type, object> _mocks;
        private readonly Expression<Action<TType>> _fieldSelector;

        public MethodVerifier(
          IDictionary<Type, object> mocks,
          Expression<Action<TType>> fieldSelector)
        {
            _mocks = mocks;
            _fieldSelector = fieldSelector;
        }

        public void WasCalled()
        {
            if (!_mocks.ContainsKey(typeof(TType)))
                throw new Exception(
                    string.Format(
                        "The requested dependency '{0}' is not specified",
                        typeof(TType).FullName));

            var mock = (Mock<TType>)_mocks[typeof(TType)];
```

```
            mock.Verify(_fieldSelector);
        }
    }

    public class ValueSetter<TType, TProperty> where TType : class
    {
        private readonly IDictionary<Type, object> _mocks;
        private readonly Expression<Func<TType, TProperty>>
            _fieldSelector;

        public ValueSetter(
            IDictionary<Type, object> mocks,
            Expression<Func<TType, TProperty>> fieldSelector)
        {
            _mocks = mocks;
            _fieldSelector = fieldSelector;
        }

        public void IsSetTo(TProperty value)
        {
            if (!_mocks.ContainsKey(typeof(TType)))
                throw new Exception(
                    string.Format(
                        "The requested dependency '{0}' is not specified",
                        typeof(TType).FullName));

            var mock = (Mock<TType>)_mocks[typeof(TType)];
            mock.SetupGet(_fieldSelector).Returns(value);
        }
    }
}
```

CQRS and Event Sourcing

By combining CQRS and Event Sourcing[20] we get an architecture that is very suitable for black box testing its behavior, which was a real eye opener when Greg demonstrated this to me. He says that the way to bring your aggregate root back into the desired state is to playback the events that are needed to do so. Then you can execute the behavior on the aggregate root, and finally to actually verify your behavior you retrieve the published events and verify that they are as expected.

Now the beauty of this is that the setup and the verification this will work on any aggregate root because we are using the IEventProvider interface there that they all implement. The only actual knowledge about the aggregate root that remains is the specific behavior that you trigger.

But I went a little bit further then what was shown during the course, I am saying that instead of executing the behavior on the aggregate root we could also just provide the command that should trigger this behavior to be executed. Because the command would be handled by a specific command handler which in turn would execute the domain behavior.

Now below here is the command test fixture that allows me to do just that, I need to provide the actual command, command handler and aggregate root types that are to be used in this specification.

```csharp
namespace Test.Fohjin.DDD
{
    [Specification]
    public abstract class CommandTestFixture<
        TCommand,
        TCommandHandler,
        TAggregateRoot>
          where TCommand : class, ICommand
          where TCommandHandler : class, ICommandHandler<TCommand>
          where TAggregateRoot : class, IOrginator,
            IEventProvider<IDomainEvent>, new()
    {
        private IDictionary<Type, object> mocks;

        protected TAggregateRoot AggregateRoot;
        protected ICommandHandler<TCommand> CommandHandler;
        protected Exception CaughtException;
        protected IEnumerable<IDomainEvent> PublishedEvents;
        protected virtual void SetupDependencies() { }
        protected virtual IEnumerable<IDomainEvent> Given()
        {
            return new List<IDomainEvent>();
```

---

[20]http://elegantcode.com/2009/11/11/cqrs-la-greg-young/

```csharp
            }
        protected virtual void Finally() { }
        protected abstract TCommand When();

        [Given]
        public void Setup()
        {
            mocks = new Dictionary<Type, object>();
            CaughtException = new NoExceptionButOneWasExpectedException();
            AggregateRoot = new TAggregateRoot();
            AggregateRoot.LoadFromHistory(Given());

            CommandHandler = BuildCommandHandler();

            SetupDependencies();
            try
            {
                CommandHandler.Execute(When());
                PublishedEvents = AggregateRoot.GetChanges();
            }
            catch (Exception exception)
            {
                CaughtException = exception;
            }
            finally
            {
                Finally();
            }
        }

        public Mock<TType> OnDependency<TType>() where TType : class
        {
            return (Mock<TType>)mocks[typeof(TType)];
        }

        private ICommandHandler<TCommand> BuildCommandHandler()
        {
            var constructorInfo = typeof(TCommandHandler)
                .GetConstructors().First();

            foreach (var parameter in constructorInfo.GetParameters())
            {
```

```csharp
                    if (parameter.ParameterType == typeof(
                       IDomainRepository<IDomainEvent>))
                    {
                        var repositoryMock = new Mock<IDomainRepository<
                          IDomainEvent>>();
                        repositoryMock.Setup(
                          x => x.GetById<TAggregateRoot>(It.IsAny<Guid>()))
                                .Returns(AggregateRoot);
                        repositoryMock.Setup(
                          x => x.Add(It.IsAny<TAggregateRoot>()))
                                .Callback<TAggregateRoot>(
                                  x => AggregateRoot = x);
                        mocks.Add(parameter.ParameterType, repositoryMock);
                        continue;
                    }

                    mocks.Add(
                      parameter.ParameterType,
                      CreateMock(parameter.ParameterType));
                }

                return (ICommandHandler<TCommand>)constructorInfo
                  .Invoke(mocks.Values.Select(
                    x => ((Mock) x).Object).ToArray());
            }

            private static object CreateMock(Type type)
            {
                var constructorInfo = typeof (Mock<>)
                  .MakeGenericType(type).GetConstructors().First();
                return constructorInfo.Invoke(new object[]{});
            }
        }

        public class ThereWasNoExceptionButOneWasExpectedException
            : Exception {}
    }
```

Please note that the Given method now returns an IEnumerable<IDomainEvent> this is to be used to provide the events that are needed to bring the aggregate root into the correct state for this specification. This is using the exact same mechanism as the actual code uses to make state changes in the aggregate root, so there cannot be a case that you are testing your aggregate root using a state that it cannot get into.

The When method returns the expected command, so all you do there is create the command with the correct information and return it to the specification.

Then in the try catch block you may have noticed that a command handler is executing the provided command and that after that the events are being retrieved from the aggregate root. These events are what you would verify to make sure your domain behavior is correct.

But this may all sound very abstract, lets look at a simple specification and see how clean and readable is really is:

```csharp
namespace Test.Fohjin.DDD.Scenarios.Withdrawing_cash
{
    public class When_withdrawing_cash : CommandTestFixture<
        WithdrawlCashCommand,
        WithdrawlCashCommandHandler,
        ActiveAccount>
    {
        protected override IEnumerable<IDomainEvent> Given()
        {
            yield return new AccountOpenedEvent(
              Guid.NewGuid(),
              Guid.NewGuid(),
              "AccountName",
              "1234567890");
            yield return new CashDepositedEvent(20, 20);
        }

        protected override WithdrawlCashCommand When()
        {
            return new WithdrawlCashCommand(Guid.NewGuid(), 5);
        }

        [Then]
        public void Then_a_cash_withdrawn_event_will_be_published()
        {
            PublishedEvents.Last().WillBeOfType<CashWithdrawnEvent>();
        }

        [Then]
        public void Then_the_event_will_contain_the_amount_and_balance()
        {
            PublishedEvents.Last<CashWithdrawnEvent>().Balance.WillBe(15);
            PublishedEvents.Last<CashWithdrawnEvent>().Amount.WillBe(5);
        }
    }
}
```

So you provide historical events to bring the aggregate root into the expected state, you fire of the command, then you verify the published events to ensure your domain behavior is correct. If you choose the correct naming for your events and commands, then a business person would be able to understand the specification. Especially if you parse the text and do a little bit of formatting.

Where is Should?

Hey what are all those WillBe and WillBeOfType things that I see in your specifications, should they not be ShouldBe and ShouldBeOfType? Well I used to think so as well, until I attended a presentation by Kevlin Henney at NDC[21] where he explained that Should is not specific enough. Should indicates that it might not. I like to use the example; "I should really do the dishes, but I won't". By using Will Be and Must you are much more dictating what will or must happen, its not a question anymore.

Finally

I am completely taken by this approach and as you see you don't need a big BDD framework for this. I think using something like this gives a good learning experience before going towards an actual BDD framework like MSpec[22]. Also Uncle Bob just wrote a good post about to not abuse the Given When Then approach[23] and also take a look at the Mocks aren't Stubs[24] article by Martin Fowler.

By now you must <grin> understand that I like to throw with code examples so yes the chapter is very long, but I hope it provides enough value instead of just confusion.

---

[21] http://arkiv.ndc2009.no/agenda.aspx?cat=1071&id=1813&day=3728
[22] http://codebetter.com/blogs/aaron.jensen/archive/2008/05/08/introducing-machine-specifications-or-mspec-for-short.aspx
[23] http://blog.objectmentor.com/articles/2009/12/19/the-polyglot-tester
[24] http://martinfowler.com/articles/mocksArentStubs.html

Using conventions with Passive View

I was reading Ayende's blog post about building UI based on conventions[25] and thought; hey I have something similar in my CQRS example[26]. And since this is the least interesting part of the whole example I guess it will be missed by many, and I can't let that happen.

Passive View

The example has a Win Forms application in there that is build accordingly to the Passive View pattern[27], so my actual forms are being dumbed down to simple views without any logic in them, well almost no logic. Then I have presenters that have the actual logic in them, or delegate the logic to other responsible entities (services or whatever).

The reason for doing this is because you want to be able to test the behavioral parts of your code as simple as possible, and nothing is more simple then being able to unit test your behavior, hey even better drive your design / behavior through Test-Driven Design (TDD). Imagine how hard that would be to do when not abstracting these different responsibilities from each other (hehe I am sure some of you don't even need to imagine this ;)).

I realize the Win Forms is so not *in* anymore and that nobody uses them, but perhaps what I show you here makes you think about other areas that this could be applied to.

The View

The view is responsible for displaying information to a user, capturing user requests, and ... uhm no that's it. Let's take a look at a simple view.

---

[25] http://ayende.com/Blog/archive/2009/12/19/effectus-building-ui-based-on-conventions.aspx
[26] http://github.com/MarkNijhof/Fohjin/tree/master/Fohjin.DDD.Example/
[27] http://martinfowler.com/eaaDev/PassiveScreen.html

```csharp
namespace Fohjin.DDD.BankApplication.Views
{
    public partial class ClientSearchForm : Form, IClientSearchFormView
    {
        public ClientSearchForm()
        {
            InitializeComponent();
            RegisterClientEvents();
        }

        public event EventAction OnCreateNewClient;
        public event EventAction OnOpenSelectedClient;

        private void RegisterClientEvents()
        {
            addANewClientToolStripMenuItem.Click +=
              (s, e) => OnCreateNewClient();
            _clients.Click += (s, e) => OnOpenSelectedClient();
        }

        public IEnumerable<ClientReport> Clients
        {
            get { return (IEnumerable<ClientReport>)_clients.DataSource; }
            set { _clients.DataSource = value; }
        }

        public ClientReport GetSelectedClient()
        {
            return (ClientReport)_clients.SelectedItem;
        }
    }
}
```

So what is happening here? As you can see there are two public events declared and there are two properties that provide access to some form controls. The interesting thing here is that the two public events are wired to two events from two form controls. But hey nothing is happening; no behavior, no calls to services or anything. Below here is the declaration of the interface that the form implements.

```csharp
namespace Fohjin.DDD.BankApplication.Views
{
    public interface IClientSearchFormView : IView
    {
        IEnumerable<ClientReport> Clients { get; set; }
        ClientReport GetSelectedClient();
        event EventAction OnCreateNewClient;
        event EventAction OnOpenSelectedClient;
    }
}
```

Here are both the two public events and the two properties that provide access to two form controls, of course the implementation could be anything. This interface is used by the presenter to control the view.

The Presenter

So the presenter is responsible for controlling the view; which includes setting and retrieving data and executing behavior that is triggered by the user of the view. Below is the presenter that is responsible for managing the previous mentioned view.

```csharp
namespace Fohjin.DDD.BankApplication.Presenters
{
    public class ClientSearchFormPresenter
        : Presenter<IClientSearchFormView>, IClientSearchFormPresenter
    {
        private readonly IClientSearchFormView _clientSearchFormView;

        public ClientSearchFormPresenter(
            IClientSearchFormView clientSearchFormView)
            : base(clientSearchFormView)
        {
            _clientSearchFormView = clientSearchFormView;
        }

        public void CreateNewClient()
        {
            // Do something
        }

        public void OpenSelectedClient()
        {
            // Do something
        }

        public void Display()
        {
            LoadData();
            try
            {
                _clientSearchFormView.ShowDialog();
            }
            finally
            {
                _clientSearchFormView.Dispose();
            }
        }
```

```
37
38          private void LoadData()
39          {
40              // Do something
41          }
42      }
43  }
```

For simplicity I removed any other external dependencies and replaced the behavior with a comment "Do something". Talking about external dependencies; the interface that is implemented by the view is injected into the presenter, this is interesting.

Look at the Display method, there you see that the view that is injected first gets its data loaded and then actually gets activated. This means that the view will not get its own data, but that the presenter will provide it to the view, for this the presenter will use the two properties that where declared in the interface. And it means that the presenter is responsible for activating the view. This is different from how Win Forms works out of the box.

For this to work I had to change the Program class, here take a look:

```csharp
namespace Fohjin.DDD.BankApplication
{
    static class Program
    {
        /// <summary>
        /// The main entry point for the application.
        /// </summary>
        [STAThread]
        static void Main()

        {
            ApplicationBootStrapper.BootStrap();

            var clientSearchFormPresenter =
                ObjectFactory.GetInstance<IClientSearchFormPresenter>();

            Application.EnableVisualStyles();

            clientSearchFormPresenter.Display();
        }
    }
}
```

Look at line 17 in there, the method Display is called on the presenter, which then prepares and activates the view.

But I can hear you think; what about these two events that where declared on that interface as well, you know "OnCreateNewClient" and "OnOpenSelectedClient"? I can see some obvious candidates "CreateNewClient" and "OpenSelectedClient" but they are not wired-up together. What gives?

The Magic

You must have noticed that the names are very similar and that they follow a certain pattern, this is the convention that I have chosen to use. Basically I call my event handlers the same as the events without the "On" prefix. Then I have a base presenter class without the word "Base" because that would be EVIL. And this class will wire-up the events with the event handlers for me.

```csharp
namespace Fohjin.DDD.BankApplication.Presenters
{
    public abstract class Presenter<TView> where TView : class, IView
    {
        protected Presenter(TView view)
        {
            HookUpViewEvents(view);
        }

        private void HookUpViewEvents(TView view)
        {
            var viewDefinedEvents = GetViewDefinedEvents();
            var viewEvents = GetViewEvents(view, viewDefinedEvents);
            var presenterEventHandlers =
              GetPresenterEventHandlers(viewDefinedEvents, this);

            foreach (var viewDefinedEvent in viewDefinedEvents)
            {
                var eventInfo = viewEvents[viewDefinedEvent];
                var methodInfo = GetTheEventHandler(
                    viewDefinedEvent, presenterEventHandlers, eventInfo);

                WireUpTheEventAndEventHandler(
                   view,
                   eventInfo,
                   methodInfo);
            }
        }

        private MethodInfo GetTheEventHandler(
          string viewDefinedEvent,
          IDictionary<string, MethodInfo> presenterEventHandlers,
          EventInfo eventInfo)
        {
            var substring = viewDefinedEvent.Substring(2);
            if (!presenterEventHandlers.ContainsKey(substring))
                throw new Exception(
                    string.Format(
                        "\n\nThere is no event handler for event '{0}' "+
                        "on presenter '{1}' expected '{2}'\n\n",
                        eventInfo.Name,
                        GetType().FullName,
```

```csharp
                substring));

        return presenterEventHandlers[substring];
    }

    private void WireUpTheEventAndEventHandler(
      TView view,
      EventInfo eventInfo,
      MethodInfo methodInfo)
    {
        var newDelegate = Delegate.CreateDelegate(
          typeof(EventAction),
          this,
          methodInfo);
        eventInfo.AddEventHandler(view, newDelegate);
    }

    private static IDictionary<string, MethodInfo>
      GetPresenterEventHandlers<TPresenter>(
        ICollection<string> actionProperties,
        TPresenter presenter)
    {
        return presenter
            .GetType()
            .GetMethods(BindingFlags.Instance | BindingFlags.Public)
            .Where(x => Contains(actionProperties, x))
            .ToList()
            .Select(x => new KeyValuePair<string, MethodInfo>(
              x.Name,
              x))
            .ToDictionary(x => x.Key, x => x.Value);
    }

    private static List<string> GetViewDefinedEvents()
    {
        return typeof(TView).GetEvents().Select(x => x.Name).ToList();
    }

    private static IDictionary<string, EventInfo> GetViewEvents(
      TView view,
      ICollection<string> actionProperties)
    {
```

```
 85            return view
 86                .GetType()
 87                .GetEvents()
 88                .Where(x => Contains(actionProperties, x))
 89                .ToList()
 90                .Select(x => new KeyValuePair<string, EventInfo>(
 91                    x.Name,
 92                    x))
 93                .ToDictionary(x => x.Key, x => x.Value);
 94        }
 95
 96        private static bool Contains(
 97            ICollection<string> actionProperties,
 98            EventInfo x)
 99        {
100            return actionProperties.Contains(x.Name);
101        }
102
103        private static bool Contains(
104            ICollection<string> actionProperties,
105            MethodInfo x)
106        {
107            return actionProperties.Contains(
108                string.Format("On{0}", x.Name));
109        }
110    }
111 }
```

The abstract base class Presenter needs the view interface as the generic parameter of the view that the presenter controls. A reference to the actual view will be injected into the presenter class. Then the first thing that happens is that I get all the events declared from the provided interface. Then I get the actual events from the provided view, but only those that have been defined on the provided interface. This makes it possible to define multiple interfaces on the same view that get controlled by different presenters. After this I get all the public methods from the presenter.

Once I have the events form the view and the methods from the presenter then I can start matching them together. As I mentioned before in my case I use a very simple convention where the event is prefixed with "On" so in order to get the event handler I only need to search my event handler collection for a name of the event minus "On". Then finally the event gets the event handler added to its collection of event handlers.

When there is no event handler for a provided event then I throw an exception, because I consider this to be a bug. There might be event handlers that does not have an event associated with it, but I consider that less harmful since this logic would not be called anyway. This exception will be visible in the unit tests for the presenter.

Reflection

Yes this relies very heavily on reflection, but for this scenario I don't mind. Indeed it is slower, but the question is; will you notice this when displaying a form, and I don't think you will. You could improve this code by for example making the WireUpEventAndEventHandler an action and cache those for the combination of the presenter and view interface, but I don't think that is worth the effort.

The Specifications

I am going to leave you with the specifications that I have for the presenter that I used for this post. The whole presenter is being tested by setting data on the view and triggering events. I am not calling the methods directly on the presenter itself. And if you want to see more, then get the code from GitHub[28].

```csharp
namespace Test.Fohjin.DDD.Scenarios.Opening_the_bank_application
{
    public class When_in_the_GUI_openeing_the_bank_application
        : PresenterTestFixture<ClientSearchFormPresenter>
    {
        private List<ClientReport> _clientReports;

        protected override void SetupDependencies()
        {
            _clientReports = new List<ClientReport> {
              new ClientReport(Guid.NewGuid(), "Client Name") };
            OnDependency<IReportingRepository>()
                .Setup(x => x.GetByExample<ClientReport>(null))
                .Returns(_clientReports);
        }

        protected override void When()
        {
            Presenter.Display();
        }

        [Then]
        public void Then_show_dialog_will_be_called_on_the_view()
        {
            On<IClientSearchFormView>().VerifyThat.Method(
                x => x.ShowDialog()).WasCalled();
        }

        [Then]
        public void Then_data_from_the_repository_is_loaded_in_view()
        {
            On<IClientSearchFormView>().VerifyThat.ValueIsSetFor(
                x => x.Clients = _clientReports);
        }
```

---

[28]http://github.com/MarkNijhof/Fohjin/tree/master/Fohjin.DDD.Example/

```
35         }
36 }
```

```csharp
1  namespace Test.Fohjin.DDD.Scenarios.Adding_a_new_client
2  {
3      public class When_in_the_GUI_adding_a_new_client
4          : PresenterTestFixture<ClientSearchFormPresenter>
5      {
6          protected override void When()
7          {
8              On<IClientSearchFormView>().FireEvent(
9                  x => x.OnCreateNewClient += delegate { });
10         }
11
12         [Then]
13         public void Then_data_from_the_repository_is_loaded_in_view()
14         {
15             On<IClientDetailsPresenter>().VerifyThat.Method(
16                 x => x.SetClient(null)).WasCalled();
17         }
18
19         [Then]
20         public void Then_display_will_be_called_on_the_view()
21         {
22             On<IClientDetailsPresenter>().VerifyThat.Method(
23                 x => x.Display()).WasCalled();
24         }
25     }
26 }
```

```csharp
1  namespace Test.Fohjin.DDD.Scenarios.Displaying_client_details
2  {
3      public class When_in_the_GUI_opening_an_existing_client
4          : PresenterTestFixture<ClientSearchFormPresenter>
5      {
6          private ClientReport _clientReport;
7
8          protected override void SetupDependencies()
9          {
10             OnDependency<IPopupPresenter>()
11                 .Setup(x => x.CatchPossibleException(It.IsAny<Action>()))
```

```csharp
                .Callback<Action>(x => x());

            _clientReport = new ClientReport(
                Guid.NewGuid(),
                "Client Name");

            OnDependency<IClientSearchFormView>()
                .Setup(x => x.GetSelectedClient())
                .Returns(_clientReport);
        }

        protected override void When()
        {
            On<IClientSearchFormView>().FireEvent(
                x => x.OnOpenSelectedClient += delegate { });
        }

        [Then]
        public void Then_get_selected_client_will_be_called_on_the_view()
        {
            On<IClientSearchFormView>().VerifyThat.Method(
                x => x.GetSelectedClient()).WasCalled();
        }

        [Then]
        public void Then_data_from_the_repository_is_loaded_in_view()
        {
            On<IClientDetailsPresenter>().VerifyThat.Method(
                x => x.SetClient(_clientReport)).WasCalled();
        }

        [Then]
        public void Then_display_will_be_called_on_the_view()
        {
            On<IClientDetailsPresenter>().VerifyThat.Method(
                x => x.Display()).WasCalled();
        }
    }
}
```

The Ubiquitous Language is not Ubiquitous

I attended an interesting Domain-Driven Design talk today given by Janniche Haugen[29] talking about why you would want to use Domain-Driven Design in a project, and this presentation is what triggered this post.

My statement is that the Ubiquitous Language in Domain-Driven Design is not Ubiquitous.

Lets first look at the definition of ubiquitous: Being present everywhere at once[30]. Hmm that sounds a bit vague; here is a definition of ubiquitous language: A language structured around the domain model and used by all team members to connect all activities of the team with the software[31]. Ah that is better. So the ubiquitous language is a common language shared by the domain experts, developers and the code.

But it is not a common language throughout all of the domain and code, this is one of the reasons why we have different bounded contexts[32]. Because the same language may mean different things to different domain experts. Think for example about a shipping company, the meaning of the word ship is completely different when talking to accounting versus maintenance. For accounting a ship is an asset that degrades in value over time, but for maintenance a ship is an object that needs service every x nautical miles.

The same word has a different meaning when used in a different context, that is not ubiquitous.

Lets continue the small example, domain experts from maintenance also talk about an engine and rotor blades. But the domain expert in accounting don't use these words at all, they have no meaning to them.

Some words even have no meaning at all when used in a different context, this as well is not ubiquitous.

So the Ubiquitous Language is only Ubiquitous within a given Context. What do you think?

---

[29]http://twitter.com/miss_haugen/
[30]http://wordnetweb.princeton.edu/perl/webwn?s=ubiquitous
[31]http://domaindrivendesign.org/node/132
[32]http://domaindrivendesign.org/node/91

Convention over Configuration

Just a quick note on Convention over Configuration, I believe this is one of the more useful practices that you can apply in your codebase. So what is this all about then? Well think of about everything you do in life; think for example about "opening a door" or "turning on the water" we all exactly know how to do those things, and because of that it is a fast action. It is something that we don't have to figure out just before doing it, again and again. These are conventions.

When we start applying these sorts of ideas to our code base this would mean that certain operations need far less thought as they will be the same each and every time. A good example here is mapping the controllers and view together and extracting the URL from the controller name in MVC. If you are a developer that knows these conventions then you know exactly where to look for the code of a certain URL. No need to figure this out each and every time.

Conventions also bring an opportunity to automate things within your system, because you are following certain rules in your code, you can write some other code that does something accordingly to these same rules. Configuration is a area that greatly benefits from conventions. Instead of having to manually configure how each different part works together you can write some code that configures this for you. You can also write some tests that verify your conventions.

Configure your Conventions

Many frameworks apply conventional thinking in their code, making it easier for their users to use it. There are frameworks like Ruby on Rails that rely very much on conventions, the only thing here is that these conventions cannot be changed very easily. This makes the framework very opinionated. This is not necessarily a bad thing in fact this means that any Ruby on Rails developer can jump to any other Ruby on Rails project and start working on it (sort of).

But frameworks that allow you to configure your own conventions are much more powerful, because not all conventions make sense in every scenario. FubuMVC is one such framework where we try not to be to opinionated (we are) so that you may configure your own conventions.

Not just for framework code

I try to figure out what conventions that are in a system that I am working on and make them explicit as soon as it makes sense. The benefits are clearly there in my eyes, being able to test them and apply them is great. This is not something you would only want to apply in framework code, for example the win forms application that I created in my CQRS example also uses conventions to hook up the views with the presenter. Very easy and I don't have to configure it manually ever again.

Now adding a new event to the application is like turning on the water or opening the door.

Trying to make it re-usable

If you have been following the source code changes on GitHub[33] you may have noticed that I renamed the folder Fohjin.DDD to Fohjin.DDD.Example, my intention is to not make anymore changes there. Instead I have created a new folder next to it and in there I am rebuilding the same components but now with re-use and ease-of-use in mind.

The first thing that is very obvious in the example code is that the domain is not very persistence ignorant, something that is valued a lot in Domain-Driven Design. So this is something that I wanted to try to address first. I really like the way NHibernate makes our code persistence ignorant and am attempting to solve this in a similar manner, using Castle DynamicProxy[34].

Since I am a complete Castle DynamicProxy noob I asked the help of Krzysztof Koźmic[35] who is an active committer on the Castle project. Krzysztof was gracias enough to get me through the basics in .Net proxy-ing. For those interested in this technology I would also recommend reading his excellent blog series[36] about the same topic.

What I want to achieve is that you get back your poco and I am going to show you one suggestion that I have working now.

For comparison I'll show you here how an aggregate root looks like in my initial example code (it is stripped down to only contain one behavioral method):

```
namespace Fohjin.DDD.Domain.Client
{
    public class Client : BaseAggregateRoot<IDomainEvent>, IOrginator
    {
        private Address _address;

        public Client()
        {
            registerEvents();
        }

        public void ClientMoved(Address newAddress)
        {
            Apply(new ClientMovedEvent(
                newAddress.Street,
                newAddress.StreetNumber,
                newAddress.PostalCode,
```

---

[33]http://github.com/MarkNijhof/Fohjin
[34]http://www.castleproject.org/dynamicproxy/index.html
[35]http://twitter.com/Kkozmic
[36]http://kozmic.pl/archive/2009/04/27/castle-dynamic-proxy-tutorial.aspx

```
18                newAddress.City));
19          }
20
21          IMemento IOrginator.CreateMemento()
22          {
23              return new ClientMemento(
24                  Id,
25                  Version,
26                  _address.Street,
27                  _address.StreetNumber,
28                  _address.PostalCode,
29                  _address.City);
30          }
31
32          void IOrginator.SetMemento(IMemento memento)
33          {
34              var clientMemento = (ClientMemento) memento;
35              Id = clientMemento.Id;
36              Version = clientMemento.Version;
37              _address = new Address(
38                  clientMemento.Street,
39                  clientMemento.StreetNumber,
40                  clientMemento.PostalCode,
41                  clientMemento.City);
42          }
43
44          private void registerEvents()
45          {
46              RegisterEvent<ClientMovedEvent>(onNewClientMoved);
47          }
48
49          private void onNewClientMoved(ClientMovedEvent clientMovedEvent)
50          {
51              _address = new Address(
52                  clientMovedEvent.Street,
53                  clientMovedEvent.StreetNumber,
54                  clientMovedEvent.PostalCode,
55                  clientMovedEvent.City);
56          }
57      }
58 }
```

And here is the same aggregate root but now *more* persistence ignorant:

```csharp
namespace Fohjin.DDD.Domain.Client
{
    public class Client
    {
        protected virtual void Apply(object @event) { }
        protected IEnumerable<Type> RegisteredEvents()
        {
            yield return typeof(ClientMovedEvent);
        }

        protected virtual Address Address { get; set; }

        public void ClientMoved(Address newAddress)
        {
            Apply(new ClientMovedEvent(newAddress));
        }
    }
}
```

Ok this may seem a bit strange at first, I mean we are sending an event into nothing and we don't set our state anymore. Let me try to explain :)

Convention over Configuration

Well in order to make this work I am going to insist on some conventions, in fact it is going to be very opinionated. If you want to learn more about convention over configuration then I would suggest reading Jeremy Millers[37] article on MSDN[38]. Personally I am all in favor for some strong guidelines so lets just go over them and see if they make sense to you as well.

Mandatory methods

The protected virtual method Apply and the protected method RegisteredEvents are both mandatory if you want to instantiate the aggregate root using this approach.

In the RegisteredEvents you return all the events that the aggregate root can publish, this is to let the persistence code know what it can expect. So when you add some new behavior that will publish a

---

[37] http://codebetter.com/blogs/jeremy.miller/
[38] http://msdn.microsoft.com/en-us/magazine/dd419655.aspx

new event then you just add it to the list here. I think that you can sort of think about this as the mapping classes in NHibernate.

The Apply method is used to publish the events from the domain behavior, but as you can see it has an empty method body, so nothing will happen, right? Here we use Castle DynamicProxy to intercept calls to this method and replace the behavior (non-existing) with our persistence logic. Where this logic comes from I'll explain in a minute.

Internal state needs to be protected virtual properties

One other difference with this approach versus the example code is that instead of private fields or private properties for the internal state, it now needs to be in the form of protected virtual properties. The reason for this is because state will not be managed by the aggregate root anymore, but instead by something that we add using Castle DynamicProxy and we will be using interception to map the properties to the internal representation of the state. The code even throws an exception if the aggregate root tries to set the internal state directly.

The event store

I haven't done anything with the event store yet, I don't think the functionality will change much from the code in the example project. One thing that will remain the same is the dependency on interfaces, and not on specific implementations. This is obviously because it is good design practices. And it will enable us to mix this new approach and the approach using the BaseAggregateRoot class together with the same event store. The BaseAggregateRoot is discussed in detail here[39].

Mix-in magic

So after reading the previous chapter you would probably say, but this aggregate root doesn't implement anything? This is true, but when our repository is instantiating the aggregate root it is also adding or injecting two more classes into it. One class that implements the IEventProvider interface and an other class that implements the IOrginator interface. This is called mixing-in classes and by doing so the aggregate root will implement both these two interfaces and it will re-direct calls to it to the mix-in classes. So as far as our event store knows it just is a class that implements the needed interfaces.

Why have everything protected?

Well in order to be able to intercept members using Castle DynamicProxy these members need to be visible to the interceptor. The most private way that is available to us is protected, and the reason

---

[39] http://elegantcode.com/2009/11/20/cqrs-the-domain-events/

why I want this to be as private as possible is because this is not domain logic, and thus should not be visible to the users of the domain. For the same reason you may notice that for example the IEventProvider implementation has all the members implement the interface explicitly thus hiding them when the domain is used and only showing them when the domain is explicitly casted to the IEventProvider interface.

I have been thinking about providing a basic interface that dictates that the Apply and RegisterEvents methods needs to be present, but I like this approach better as from the outside these implementation details would not be known, but I could imagine being able to support both approaches.

Reflect only once

There is quite a bit of reflection going on to discover and the properties of both the domain events and the aggregate root internal state. But once this is done once the results will be cached and re-used for each sequential need. But I am sure this can improve quite a bit :)

Conventional limits

So what if I run into the limits of this conventional approach? Well the Event Store only cares about that the different interfaces are implemented, so you will be able to switch back to the BaseAggregateRoot solution at any time. This does mean that you will have to do some more coding, but you will have all the freedom to do what ever you need to do. And the different approaches can be used side by side.

One other limit is that if you instantiate the aggregate root yourself nothing will be intercepted and mixed-in so no state will change nor will the events be published.

Current state

Currently the code only supports very basic usages and there are some challenges ahead of it being truly useable. Think for example about other entities in the same aggregate managed by the aggregate root and collecting their events as well. Also think about adding and removing entities from a list which may need some configurable conventions so you can decide when something needs to be added or removed.

I am thinking about the ability to provide adapters to be able to handle certain state changes differently from the conventional way. One that I see a need for already is the ability to set the aggregate root Id, since this is not managed by the aggregate root but by the event provider mix-in.

Finally

Currently the functionality is very limited but I have tests passing proving that this is working :) so what I would like is to get some feedback on this approach. And yes I realize that this is very opinionated, and will not fit everybody's approach. Having said that, keep the suggestions coming anyway.

Printed in Poland
by Amazon Fulfillment
Poland Sp. z o.o., Wrocław